"My Number Was Up, Dad"

GARY VAUGHT

Bloomington, IN  Milton Keynes, UK

authorHOUSE®

AuthorHouse™
1663 Liberty Drive, Suite 200
Bloomington, IN 47403
www.authorhouse.com
Phone: 1-800-839-8640

AuthorHouse™ UK Ltd.
500 Avebury Boulevard
Central Milton Keynes, MK9 2BE
www.authorhouse.co.uk
Phone: 08001974150

First published by AuthorHouse 8/1/2006

ISBN: 1-4259-3786-1 (sc)
ISBN: 1-4259-3785-3 (dj)

Library of Congress Control Number: 2006907040

Printed in the United States of America
Bloomington, Indiana

This book is printed on acid-free paper.

Dedications

As of this date, prior to publication, my wife has yet to read this story. She doesn't feel it is necessary because she has lived it in its entirety. Still, for all of the pain and suffering that she has endured, her emotional resilience has been nothing short of extraordinary. This book I dedicate to her loving ways and her wonderful parenting with both of our children!

The fact that she also delivered so many of the early messages from Gabriel further reinforces her heartfelt love and compassion, when so often she was unable to recall the beauty, the divine message, or even the laughter enjoyed with so many of the conversations that she channeled, mostly on my behalf. How fortunate Gabe was, and Noah is, to have had this much inspiration and security in one so beautiful as Mom.

To my wonderful and blessed son, Noah, I send our greatest love and appreciation for your caring, your support, and willingness to do all that you could to comfort us during our extreme emotional grief. Knowing how sad and real the grief was for you, too, this made the demonstration of your commitment and love to us all the more extraordinary. We are blessed to have you and to know you as our son. The world is blessed to have you as a creator of many exceptional thoughts and ideas. Stay the course, son! Your greatness lays in your understanding of how to fulfill your hearts desires while doing the same for others at all times.

And for the support of all of the wonderful people who have rallied around us, from the Church Federation of Greater Indianapolis and Reverend Dr. Angelique Walker-Smith, I give my greatest and most sincere appreciation for all the love and kindness that you have shown us. Reverend Dr. Walker-Smith delivered a eulogy that was fit for an angel and blessed by the King.

To Ms. Kim Zimmerman, Nate Karimanski, and Marcos Dominguez; I say thank you from the bottom of our hearts for the touching seven-minute audio and video tribute to Gabe. You were Gabe's closest classmates and friends at Lawrence North High School, and we will always be grateful for the kind words and program that you produced for his service. He looks down upon you now and smiles, I assure you. But, he has told us that he is with you a great deal of the time, too. Look for signs of him – he'll be there when you call him – or simply when you think of him in your thoughts from time to time.

To my sister Pam, I dedicate this book, as well; not because she played such a significant part in it, but because she made me promise to do this from her place in paradise. Pam...I kept my word!

I want to acknowledge the deep love and respect that I have for my parents and their trials with this tragedy and turn of events.. At eighty years young, it can be a life altering event when you lose someone who is so special to you. Through their tears, I have seen uncompromising poise, grace, and grief, yet never once have I seen the face of hopelessness on either one. They know that "this, too, shall pass." It has, and we are all stronger for having faced it together. Their willingness to explore the afterlife now lends hope to so many who claim that they cannot change! My parents are learning more each day.

I hope my brothers, my sister, my in-laws, and certain members of my extended family can appreciate the courage that it has taken for us to openly discuss these revelations with them, knowing that, for some, their religious beliefs prohibit them from accepting these facts. I will not judge your positions on this. You are my family, my loved ones, and this does not change that fact or the importance of your place in our lives.

Finally, for Bill Green, Dan Stenger, Dan Hall, and their families; I thank you for your love, support, and friendship in our countless hours of need. Bill, I owe you more than I can ever pay you. My sincere, heartfelt thanks will have to do!

To all of SXU; everyone of you who observed and remembered Gabe's life and death, God bless you all!

Table of Contents

Foreword

In an age when the unknown or relative unknown is still viewed as suspicious, and evidence is only that which can be proven or has meaning by credibility, the information contained herein will, with a doubt, raise some eyebrows and reconsideration for many.

The hope is that it will raise the level of conscious thought about why we treat the relative unknown with such disrespect, when the relative unknown comprises the greatest amount of information that exists to all of time. In other words, we know so very little, as human beings, of what truly exists in our universe to any degree, that this lack of knowledge is much like a pebble on a beach full of sand, compared with that which we have yet to learn and cannot understand.

And though we accept many things that we can not know or understand the certainty of, such as who created God; how the world was created; how man was created; how angels exist; or what lies beyond our realm of scientific knowledge with the existence of billions of other galaxies in the universe that we think of; *afterlife communications* are still disregarded or accepted as real or meaningful by many non-believers. **Why?**

Such non-believers too often write off what they do not know about and/or cannot comprehend as schizophrenia or deception. It is sad, because, if we, as human beings, do this with all that we cannot know or understand, we will face a serious limitation to our human potential for growth for many decades or centuries to come, perhaps.

Divine Intervention is still unbelievable for many. Those things that cannot be directly viewed by the human sense of sight are often held by skeptics as unlikely or a figment of someone's creative imagination. Why? Why is it that we cannot see the wind, but we can and do accept it as a real part of our existence? And, yet, we cannot accept the reality of eternal life and spiritual communications from elsewhere?

What separates our ability to accept some things and not others? Is it the prior life-development programming that we learned from someone we likely trusted, but who also lacked the knowledge and awareness of the existence of many things in the universe?

My Number Was Up, Dad" is a true-life story of tragedy and then inspiration of a young man going about his daily life, like most eighteen-year-olds, attending college in Chicago, when he suddenly was taken from this earth by natural causes. The uncertainty will never be determined by exact scientific evidence as to the specific cause of death

What is more important, however, is what the death of Gabriel means to the lives of others now, and what we are to learn from his death and our life continuation here.

In an amazing and unforgettable chapter of his eternal life, two days following his death, Gabriel Vaught contacted his parents to speak to them through the eyes of a wise soul who had just completed an extraordinary journey from earth to "the other side."

His insights are spectacular, his revelations about his life, his death, the journey "beyond," and the earth world and afterlife today are even more incredible.

Recordings of conversations with him that detail different aspects of life here and on the "other side," through enlightened dialogue mostly with his Dad, are more than food for thought and nourishment for the soul. They reinforce the existence of the *"afterlife consciousness theory."* Whether one can reach the Light of the afterlife and still communicate with earthlings through a certain level of advanced consciousness is now known by the messages contained from this remarkable living story.

Gabriel Vaught lived his life on earth with a chronic illness that few really understand (diabetes). Through his handicap, he made more than friends along the way. He set examples for others on how to live with a God-centered constitution. He had the highest regard for those who were less fortunate or handicapped themselves.

After physical death, he speaks of what true friendships are and how love is the blessed force of the essence of God Almighty. He speaks of what God means to our daily living; and what our lives are and can potentially be by learning of things we do not fully grasp now.

He speaks to the hopes of every parent that has ever lost a child, to any person who has ever lost a loved one, that one day we can have the opportunity to understand much better why the death of our loved one(s) occur and what its relevance is to the lives of so many who treasured them, loved them, and still grieve for their death and our loss of our loved one(s).

He confirms that which we all have wondered about following a loved one's passing: Do supernatural spiritual or divine communications really exist, and if so, how? Can anyone speak to a loved one on the "other side?" Are we aware of where our deceased loved ones live and what they choose to do now with their eternal life?

So many questions are answered through the Essence and Grace of God, through quantum physical spiritual afterlife communications that are unknown yet, in entirety, to our scientific world.

This is a story you won't want to "put down," literally or figuratively!

Today the conversations still continue. Some people still raise their eyebrows and cough at the mention of afterlife communications. Still questioning the very thought that anyone who has died would have the capability of discussing with earthlings the Cubs, the Pacers, relatives in Heaven, or more serious subject matters that still have a significant affect on life today and in our future, here on earth!

Much of the information shared in this book, in fact, belonged to the other side, until it was granted through these afterlife discussions with Gary Vaught, through the spiritual channeling still unknown and unrevealed to scientists today.

Progressive and intimate weekly conversations that still bring about previously unknown information on life, here and hereafter, take place today with a mission for Gabe's dad:

"To learn and go forth to serve God and the divine truths as they are presented and interpreted" for passage to others to learn from, if they so choose to do so.

Through divine messages and conversations, Gabriel Vaught offers real-life (afterlife) observations and perspectives into questions that so many have wondered about for so long.

These "afterlife" messages can and will greatly affect your life here on earth. The messages are for everyone who will listen and not just for those who can see, read, or hear.

You will cry, contemplate, smile, laugh, and cry again, perhaps. But you will never be able to say "I don't know" again! ***Perhaps, your time has come to choose between believing or not believing.*** Your future education and awareness to bring about your future thinking processes, (advancing your destiny), will be, in no small part, affected by this decision you must make after reading this remarkable story.

This is an educational journey of a lifetime that takes you through the real-life events leading up to the day that Gabriel died, through the present day, where he serves the divine universe with his work.

The tale of this real life family from Fishers, Indiana, is an ongoing saga that promises to deliver more factual and previously unknown information than one could possibly think about or imagine, previously.

But, your decision, as to what you choose to believe or choose not to believe, will impact your life, forever. The lessons and knowledge are here for the taking, if you choose to believe. *Decide for yourself, based on the extraordinary information provided in these communications, how you want to view the terms for your life, and then how you want to live your life, for your remaining years here on earth.*

Whatever you decide, that is where you are and you need to accept that position as your place in this lifetime, at least for now, anyway.

First, allow the story to unfold! Your life and eternal life perceptions and thoughts are about to be tested! You are about to learn what one spirits purpose was and is and the importance and value of what a spiritual commitment to your growth means here on earth!

CHAPTER ONE

On Friday, April 23, 2004, a rainy spring day, my wife and I waited patiently for our son Gabriel to pull up in our driveway after having been away for what seemed like an eternity. He was attending college at Saint Xavier University in Chicago. Sometimes he had a long drive on the congested interstate from Chicago to our home in Indianapolis, Indiana, a journey that could take every bit of three and a half hours when traffic was heavy. But on this night, I knew something was very wrong.

So many times Gabe would telephone us the night before he was to come home, in anticipation of seeing his family and friends. It was his freshman year, and his first full year ever away from us. As an insulin-dependent diabetic, Gabe had to manage his nutritional habits, exercise program, and the sleep and rest patterns in his daily life. We worried about his ability to do this on his own. For a Type-1 diabetic like Gabe, any imbalance could cause huge swings in blood glucose levels.

Our son, Gabriel Keith Logan Vaught, was diagnosed at the age of three with diabetes. He was immediately hospitalized for several days, while his mother Dawn and I had to become experts overnight on how to care for an insulin-dependent diabetic child. My wife bought book after book on the subject to learn all she could about the chronic illness and its effects. During adolescence, children's hormones are naturally out of control a good deal of the time due to their physical growth and development. Add to that another growth hormone in insulin, and although it is a lifesaver for all Type-1 diabetics, it has side effects just like any other medication. The effects can vary at different times of the day depending on the type of insulin injected, the amount taken with each shot, and the frequency of daily injections, along with other factors that can alter glucose levels. Very seldom are any two days alike ... once in a while, but not often in the life of a young person.

At 11:00 AM on that Friday in April, I suddenly got an urge to call Gabe from work. Whenever I knew he was driving home from college, I would caution him about the road conditions, the weather, and traffic problems, but frankly ... I just loved to hear his voice and know that he was all right. As a rule, he carried his cell phone with him wherever he went. Sometimes he would forget it and leave it in his room or at someone else's place, and he made it a point to shut the phone off during his classes. So when I would get his voice message service, I always told him to call me back as soon as possible. That way I would know that he had made it successfully through another night. For a Type-1 diabetic, that is a much greater accomplishment than what it might otherwise seem to be. Every facet of your life as a diabetic becomes part of a concert within your body that is either very much in tune with your natural self, or madly out of tune, a trigger for all kinds of irrational or peculiar behavior — behavior that many times includes depression, anger, volatility, lethargy, disorientation, drowsiness, constipation, stomach ache, or migraine headaches, just to name a few of the complications brought on by hyperglycemia (high blood sugars) or hypoglycemia (low blood sugars).

I had last spoken to Gabe on Wednesday evening, April 21, for nine minutes, according to our telephone records discovered more than a month later. All that I recall about that conversation is that he planned to come back home early on Friday afternoon after an interview he had about a summer job moving furniture. It paid twenty-seven dollars an hour! Gabe was thrilled to think about how much money he could save in one summer by working at this position.

Gabe never returned my 11:00 AM telephone call on that Friday, and I assumed it was because he was quite busy, between spending time with friends, visiting record stores as he liked to do, and the job interview. Around three o'clock that afternoon, I could wait no longer. I left another anxious message on his cell phone, stating in a stern voice that I expected a call back ASAP!

Five thirty rolled around and we still had not heard from him. My wife suggested that we give him a bit more time as he probably began working that very day at the job. Still, my instincts told me that all was not right. Something was preventing him from calling us.

Just three weeks earlier, I had phoned Gabe on a day when I wanted to speak with him, and had not received a call back within the hour. At that time, my mind and heart told me to wait no longer, and I took an aggressive stance by calling the school switchboard and asking them to alert the resident assistant at Regina Hall, his dormitory. I also called Regina Hall and demanded that the operator have someone go to Gabe's room and pound on the door to get his attention. I even phoned the radio station WXAV — where Gabe was a DJ and loved to hang out, working on his radio show — and asked the station manager if they could track him down for us.

Ten minutes later, my son had called back, snapping at me about why I had to send people to find him. On that occasion, I didn't have the heart to tell him that I was worried sick that he might have lapsed into a diabetic coma and that I envisioned the possibility that he was lying unconscious in his room. It had worried me when Gabe's roommate had dropped out of school, which meant that he was often alone in the dorm. Fifteen minutes later, my wife received a call from our angry son, warning her that his father had better never do that again, because a stream of people had shown up at his room all within minutes of each other to make certain he was okay and to inform him that he needed to call home to his father. Since he had been on his cell phone chatting with his latest girlfriend, this was embarrassing and humiliating to him.

I had thus been scolded by my son for caring enough to check up on his health and well-being, when the very reason he had chosen an out-of-state school was to prove that he could finally manage his diabetes and his other affairs on his own, without his parents' constant intervention.

Gabe loved his independence. For our part, it was also the first time in his life that we had ever had the courage to allow him these freedoms. Diabetes was a dangerous disease. We were well-aware of the risks from the repeated warnings we had received during our monthly, quarterly, and annual physical examinations with his endocrinologists.

We had micromanaged the process throughout his young life without making too much of it, until he began to resist the regimen in his teens. Dawn took the day shift from 6:00 AM through 9:00 PM, though I had made several trips to school to comfort teachers, nurses, and Gabe, when close calls occurred with insulin reactions.

I took every night shift, from 9:00 PM through 6:00 AM. This meant rising anywhere from once to four times a night at different intervals to test his blood glucose levels for stability and normalcy. Ninety percent of the time throughout his entire life, there was no stability or normalcy during the nighttime hours. Exercise, nutrition, sweets, and carbohydrate and protein intake all juggled his blood sugars and left them either dangling on the edge of comatose or so high that it required staying up with him to make certain that we brought the sugars down gradually in stages, and not all at once, which can be very dangerous when the sugars measure 500 or higher. A normal range is 80-120 for a healthy human being.

In any event, managing a chronic illness such as diabetes Type-1 (insulin dependency) required a daily regimen of activity from first thing in the morning through the night, particularly during times of illness, when all-night vigils were the norm. Illness played havoc with Gabe's glucose levels. Continuous monitoring every fifteen to twenty minutes was the only means of knowing where his levels were if we were to ensure proper treatment.

Once our son had been diagnosed with diabetes, there was never a time that we felt comfortable with any type of daily routine. The truth is there is no such thing as two days that are just alike. The processes for managing each day are similar in many ways, but one small change or one small difference in diet, exercise, stress, fatigue, or hormonal balance could mean a life-threatening situation at any time.

We knew this, had experienced this on many different levels, and respected what each hour meant for Gabe's condition and his chances for a normal life. Just the slightest difference or change meant a whole new approach to the amount of insulin or the timing of eating or resting patterns during the day. For anyone not aware of the acute and chronic aspects of this insidious disease, this would have been nearly an overwhelming task to undertake. An extraordinary number of factors influenced the calculation of what adjustments needed to be made every segment of every day.

Endocrinologists hardly understand all the factors that disrupt the consistency of glucose patterns, causing extreme highs or lows to occur. Adrenalin, for example, can push glucose levels as high as two to three hundred points in a matter of half an hour. Roller coaster rides, automobile accidents, bicycle accidents, or any type of fear-driven event, could pull the trigger on a loaded gun, firing a bullet into the chemistry of the body.

When I telephoned our son again with no response, the intuition that I had always shared with my son (a joining of the minds more than anything else) kept telling me that something was wrong. At 8:00 PM, my father phoned us, very concerned about where Gabe was. He, too, was looking forward with anticipation to his grandson's visit. My father had been in poor health for several years, and his level of concern seemed unusual, yet I did everything I could to reassure him that Gabe was fine and that he probably had just got sidetracked.

When 11:00 PM came, I could wait no longer. I phoned the receptionist at Regina Hall and asked them to have security check Gabe's room to see if he might somehow still be there. The young receptionist, Patricia, sounded kind and considerate, and yet very nervous. The concern in my voice may have startled her. In any event, she said she would call me back after they had checked Gabe's room.

Within ten minutes, she phoned to say, "Mr. Vaught, you better get up here; something is very wrong."

I dashed to put my clothes on and awakened my wife, who had gone to bed, to tell her to get dressed immediately and join me in the car. I told her that it was likely that Gabe was in a diabetic coma. This had always been our greatest fear. Once he lapsed into a coma, it was anyone's guess if he would ever come out of it. And even if he did, it was not certain he would ever be the same again.

We took my Corvette and raced through the city and onto the interstate, traveling anywhere from eighty to ninety-five miles per hour for the first hour, all the while cautiously watching for state police vehicles along the way. We couldn't afford the slightest delay. Every five to ten minutes, I phoned the receptionist, Patricia, for updates. She was always caring and helpful, but not terribly informative. Each time I called, she became more anxious and uncomfortable with my requests for information about our son's condition.

In between those calls, I phoned my older sister, Donna, in Tipton, Indiana, and got her out of bed and told her that Gabe was in trouble and might not make it. She was crying and in denial but I instructed her to drive the thirty minutes south to Mom and Dad's home. Mom is seventy-nine and Dad, eighty-two; he has been on oxygen for four years since his last bypass surgery. I wanted Donna to be with them when I phoned to let them know of Gabe's condition.

I also phoned my older brother, Don, and his wife, Susan, who is a registered nurse, and asked them if they would go over to Mom and Dad's to be there in case the worst should happen. They agreed.

I suspected the worst. Otherwise, why would it take an hour to determine Gabe's condition while he was still at the dormitory where medics where reportedly working on him? Finally, I reached Patricia for a sixth time from the road on my cell phone.

"Patricia, I am his father," I said, my voice rising. "I deserve to know what is going on here. I want an answer!"

My wife sat motionless in the passenger's seat as if she could not bear to hear any news they might have to report at that moment.

"What is wrong with my son?" I demanded.

Patricia began sobbing quietly and handed the phone to a John Pelrine, who introduced himself to me.

Gabe at the traditional Easter time egg coloring preparation at home

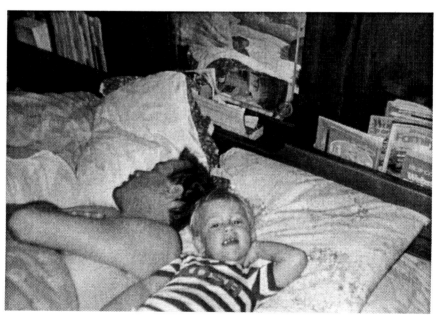

Dad's attempt to sleep in on Saturday morning foiled again by Gabe!

CHAPTER TWO

Circumstances of Notification

John Pelrine had the unenviable task of being awakened in the night and brought to the school only to learn that he was the one chosen to break the news to us about our son.

"Mr. Vaught," he stated, "my name is John Pelrine and I am the director of student services here at Saint Xavier. I have some very bad news for you, sir."

My heart stopped at that instant while driving ninety-five miles per hour near Lafayette, Indiana on I-65 headed north to Chicago. It seemed as though all time stopped at that moment … and he didn't really have to say anything else, though he did.

"Your son is dead."

At those words, I gently lifted my foot off the accelerator and tried to compose myself, mostly for my wife's sake. I stared straight ahead at the roadway.

After saying a few words to John, I confirmed that we would be there about 2:30 AM, then ended the call and placed the phone on my lap. I looked over at my wife and she said nothing for a moment.

"Gabe is dead," I told her.

She was in a state of shock, just as I was … and no doubt in unimaginable terror and denial. She then began frantically sobbing. I could only keep pressing on to Chicago with the knowledge now that our son was dead. Not how he died or why he had died. I told myself I had to get us there as soon as possible. We had to know the details. We had to see our son to believe this.

Our first call was to our other son, Noah. Noah, my wife's son by her first marriage, had just turned thirty. I have had Noah in my life since he was eight. Many years of resistance by him, and improper parenting by me, treating him as my own when he was not, did some damage to our friendship. Fortunately, we learned that we both wanted only the best for one another and I call him "son" now without any hesitation and he takes no exception to it any longer.

I handed the phone to Dawn and asked her to give the news to Noah. I didn't feel I should be the one to do this. After Dawn broke the news to Noah through her tears, Noah asked what to do next. Dawn handed the phone back to me and I asked him to come to Chicago as early as possible that same morning. He later caught a flight and arrived at 6:45 AM in Chicago and came directly to meet us at the hotel. We needed to hold him and talk with him. Noah was such a blessing for us both, particularly his mother, who was sinking deeper and deeper into despair.

For the next two and half hours on the road to Chicago, my wife and I both cried and held each other, trying in vain to ease the emptiness that we felt. We desperately wanted to see Gabe, to touch him, to hold him, and to kiss him and bring him back to life.

When I could compose myself, however slightly, I phoned my sister Donna and told her that Gabe had died. She couldn't accept it at first, then it sank in, as she realized that it would be her duty to inform my parents and the rest of the family.

My parents loved Gabe every bit as much as we did. While Gabe was growing up, we lived less than two miles away from them. Papaw and Mamaw Vaught babysat for Gabe three or four times a week when he was young.

The news could be fatal for one or both of them. Just three years earlier, my older sister, Pam, had died from lung cancer after a long and excruciating illness. It took a lot out of both of my parents. This could be the final chapter of their lives for all I knew.

I was in such a state of shock that even though I had made that same trip some forty or fifty times, I missed the I-80/I-94 West exit and didn't realize it until I got to the end of I-65 and suddenly, there was only the Indiana Toll Road exit. Confused and uncertain of what to do, I hopped on the Toll Road and went to the first pay booth where I asked for directions to Cicero Avenue and 103rd Street in Chicago.

Fortunately, although the middle of the night now, the toll booth attendant was alert and gave me directions. Somehow, we managed to make it to the University by around 2:30 AM.

When I pulled up outside Regina Hall, there were campus security guards all around, an ambulance, Chicago police officers, school administrators, and a good number of students with blank expressions on their faces. All, it seemed, were waiting for our arrival.

Slowly, my wife and I climbed out of the vehicle, no longer crying, and approached one of the security guards standing nearby.

"Are you Mr. and Mrs. Vaught?" he asked us in a steady voice.

I answered yes, and the guard nodded to a gentleman who approached and asked us if we wanted to see Gabriel, as he was no longer in his room but had been placed in the ambulance, ready to be transported to the Chicago medical examiner's office downtown.

Without any hesitation, we both replied, "Yes!" Reluctantly, haltingly, we followed as we were led toward the rear of the ambulance where two Chicago PD officers stood, one at the rear door and the other back a few feet.

The gentleman who had greeted us said: "I am so sorry . . . . Are you sure you want to view the body here, or would you rather do so downtown?"

"We want to view our son now," we told him.

For that one instant, I prayed that somehow it wouldn't truly be him. I don't know why I thought about this, but it was one last chance, I suppose, to avoid the reality of this terrible nightmare.

The police officer opened the door firmly and slid the gurney out about four feet. He unzipped the black body bag about five inches, and for the first and last time, my wife and I saw our son lying dead in a natural state. Gabe looked to us as if he were only sleeping. Then I realized there was a considerable amount of foam that had built up on his lips from an apparent attempt by the paramedics to revive him at the scene.

My wife and I stared at his precious face and hair for maybe ten seconds, then turned to one another and cried like never before. We held on to one another while walking with the school officials, and I looked momentarily to see a CPD female officer near tears also. Somehow, everyone's love and compassion there was of great comfort despite our unexplainable grief.

The ambulance pulled away with our son. I turned and walked toward the front of the building to enter, without any thought as to why I would need to go in now. My wife simply clutched my right arm and held on while I guided her with me. We went into a small office in the dormitory and tried to make sense of what had happened.

By that time, we had met Dr. Steven Murphy, the vice president of student services. He and John Pelrine were so considerate, so loving, and so kind and compassionate, even though they were visibly distraught over this whole matter themselves. But somehow, they remained poised and professional enough to offer us whatever assistance they could.

Dr. Murphy spoke several times, as did John, and all that I recall is asking them how long our son had been dead before his body was discovered. The best that John could do was estimate that several hours must have passed; it was possible that Gabe had died between three or four in the afternoon. I tried to remember where I was at that hour and think about what I might have done differently that could have saved his life. But there were no easy answers at that moment.

We were soon to be greeted by a Chicago police detective who gave us his card for identification purposes. He stated that he was in charge of the investigation, and at this time really didn't have much in the way of answers. We could travel downtown to the ME's office, he said, either now or in the morning. Then we might be able to learn a good deal more perhaps.

By this time, it was three-thirty in the morning and we were so emotionally exhausted by the night's events that we were virtually paralyzed. If it had not been for Dr. Murphy leading us a short distance from the university to the Hilton Hotel where we stayed that evening, I may have wandered around Chicago for hours afterwards.

We checked in at the Hilton. I asked for a room next to one that was vacant, for I knew we would be up all night crying and I didn't want anyone else to have to bear the burden with us.

The hotel accommodated our request. Once we entered the room and bolted the door, we cried and cried and cried until we could hardly breathe any longer. My wife was traumatized to the point that she was mostly numb by now. I was acting far too rational — my way of coping — and began placing calls to the family to let them know the grim news.

I had no idea how else to proceed. And I knew my family desperately wanted details and information. When I phoned my parents home at 4:00 AM, my niece, Kim, Donna's daughter, answered.

"Its Uncle Gary!" she shouted on the other end of the line.

"Kim," I said to her earnestly, "please tell me how Mammaw and Pappaw Vaught are doing."

"Not very well" was the reply. "When my mom told Mammaw, she went into the storage room next to the kitchen and let out a scream and cried like we've never heard her cry before!"

I couldn't bear to hear this. In that same storage room are large pictures of Gabe as a three-year-old sleeping with Pappaw in a recliner out back on the patio on a beautiful fall day, each with the same colored jacket, hat, jeans, and shoes on. The two of them were nearly inseparable for most of Gabe's childhood, it seemed. Gabe loved his grandparents so much. He called them at least once a week from college. Every opportunity to see them was special to Gabe and he made my parents feel that way whenever he came around.

Sleep seemed impossible that night. My heart pounded so hard for so long that I honestly thought about calling an ambulance. I feared that I could not take it much longer. Finally, I said a prayer and calmed my body down and stopped the flow of adrenaline long enough to close my eyes. My wife cried herself to sleep. We both did, actually.

I remember looking at my watch, and it read 4:30 AM. That was the last time I opened my eyes again until 6:15. The early morning sun shone brightly through our hotel curtains even though the night before it had rained all night menacingly. Today was a new day.

I showered and dressed, and at 7:00 AM, the hotel phone rang. I answered it and on the other end a female voice spoke in soothing tones.

"Mr. Vaught, this is Judith Dwyer, president of Saint Xavier University,"

I attempted to speak some words out of courtesy, but wasn't really sure what the call was regarding.

"I am just so heartbroken about your son's death," she went on to say, "and our community's loss. From everything I have been told, your son was loved by so many. I cannot tell you how sad we are and how much we feel for you, other than to offer to you our assistance in any way that we can to help you through this, now or in the future."

I was quite stunned by her sincerity, her heartfelt desire to offer us compassion and help, and her willingness to call so early in the morning to let us know she was thinking of us.

She went on to say that she wanted to meet with us in the near future, but right now, she simply wanted to know what the university could do to help us. I told her that we appreciated her thoughtfulness, but we simply wanted to go to Gabe's room first thing this morning to clean out his belongings and take them home with us. That was all we really could think to do … take a part of our son home with us by taking his few and most precious possessions with us.

By 8:00 AM, Bill Green, my good friend and attorney, had arrived from Crawfordsville, Indiana. Upon learning of Gabe's death, Bill had made the three-hour drive to Chicago, to be there to help us in any way he could, and to lend us support. He called us for directions and we told him to meet us over at our son's dormitory room.

We took the liberty of heading over to Regina Hall at the university, where we pulled up in front to a solemnly quiet place. Although the day was starting out so beautifully, we were as depressed as we could humanly be. We organized our thoughts quickly, however, and headed for our son's room.

The security guards let us in. They cried and attempted to comfort us while we proceeded to do the same with one another as we started going through Gabe's possessions, which, by this time, had been fairly scattered all over his room. Between our son's normal untidiness and the detective's investigation to rule out foul play or possible substance abuse, the room looked as though it had been burglarized repeatedly.

We began with my wife Dawn and me picking up any and all loose papers from the floor, sorting through any notes or letters that might have left clues or just some expression of love to us from our son. Anything was worth touching, feeling, reading, sensing, and crying over. Each handwritten note, however meaningless to any other human being now, was priceless to us.

Then Bill Green appeared, tears streaming down his face, and he pitched in with moving Gabe's possessions. It was all any of us could do to remain productive and keep moving all Gabe's belongings instead of questioning anyone and everyone in the building, hoping to find some clue to the mystery of Gabe's death. Before long, an unusually handsome, strong, chiseled-bodied, young African-American man appeared in the doorway. He was wearing a do-rag and glasses. He asked if we were Gabe's parents. After we nodded yes, he extended his hand.

"Hi, I'm Keenan Wells," said the young man. "I don't know if Gabe told you about me or not, but we were best friends."

I didn't want to act uninformed at that moment, but while I remembered Keenan's name being mentioned once or twice, I didn't really know anything about his friendship with Gabe. Still, I wasn't about to dishonor anyone, least of all this young man who had evidently been up all night crying himself, just as we had.

"Gabe and I first met when he started college here, about the second week or so," explained Keenan. "Gabe asked me about myself and I told him 'bout my past and where I came from … that kinda stuff. We just hit it off. One night, we were in his room listening to music, and I told him I had to get a ride to the train station to catch da train downtown where I worked as a night security guard. I have to work to support some of my school costs, my life, my two kids, and others.

"Gabe offered to drive me to the train station," Keenan proceeded to tell us, "and I paid for his gas for a while when he did this. But then after a while, he realized I barely had 'nuff money to get by and he quit asking me for anything at all. He would even take me all the way downtown Chicago sometimes and pick me up when I got off real late in the night. We'd just go cruising around downtown and talking about what we wanted for our lives."

I listened as Keenan, in silence, seemed unsure of what else to say.

"Mr. Vaught, if it hadn't been for your son, I would have never been able to make it to work on time or as often and I would have probably lost my job. I may not have been able to stay in school. He knew this and we had a pact! We agreed that we were both gonna make it big someday … and when we did, then we were gonna help one another big-time! I believe your son was an angel," he continued, "sent here to help me, Mr. Vaught … I really do. He was like a brother to me!"

The large, muscular black man stopped to sob softly, his eyes gazing down. Slowly, he started to shuffle away, then turned back, and softly said:

"Mr. Vaught, he might have been higher than an angel …I don't know."

Then Keenan walked off with his head down, tears streaming from his eyes. Later that day, we discovered a voice mail that Keenan had left about 3:00 AM, the morning after learning of Gabe's passing. His voice mail talked about keeping his agreements and how Gabe was like a brother to him. And he would always treasure the time they had together…and the love and brotherhood that they shared. By the time the following day came upon us, Gabe had thirty-seven unanswered voice messages from friends and people who did not know yet of his death. Several were from Keenan, however.

Brother Noah, Gabe, and Dad, all dressed up for Easter services

all dressed up as his favorite "Ninja Turtle" at Halloween

CHAPTER THREE

The Hours and Days Following Gabe's Death

As Gabe's mother and I started on the long drive back home from Chicago around noon on Saturday, the twenty-fourth of April, 2004, we were still in a complete state of shock. Amid all the confusing thoughts, images, and reflections, our minds were trying to sort out what our lives were going to be like from moment to moment without our son. I could not only not fathom this but had no understanding of how I could ever go on living with any real purpose from that time forward for the rest of my life.

During the ride on Interstate 65 between Chicago and Merrillville, Indiana, where we always stopped off to grab a bite to eat, use the restroom, and fill the tank up with gas, we tried our best to discuss any and all collection of thought as it related to what we had just experienced during the previous twelve-hour period. It was as if we were caught in a time warp. Those twelve hours seemed more like two or three days, so much emotional, mental, and spiritual trauma had occurred. At the same time, because we had everything that Gabe had taken to school with us now, there was a sense of relief that we were completing a mission. It was an odd experience, an odd feeling, and one that is hard to describe, even today.

Dawn was so exhausted and traumatized by the events that she had a look of mental abandonment on her face virtually the entire trip back. I'm not sure where she was mentally or how she was able to converse with me in any significant way, but she did. Our son Noah had flown up from Indianapolis, and he was driving Gabe's 1999 Honda Accord back with the car full of Gabe's belongings. Bill Green had driven to Chicago and his car was filled with Gabe's things, too. Gabe had acquired more usable possessions, most of which he truly needed for some purpose and used regularly in his life, than most middle-aged married couples accumulate and store as pack rats for sentimental purposes.

When we got to Merrillville, we stopped off and ate at a small steak house. All I remember is feeling as though I needed to eat a bite, yet at the same time, being numb, emotionally exhausted, and not really hungry. I looked over at my wife, and tears were softly rolling down her cheek as she attempted to wipe them away, to show her courage.

After lunch, we climbed back in the car for the journey home, and I asked Dawn if she would like to take a nap, which she agreed to do. At that time, I began to ponder all the dramatic events of the past day. An hour or so later, we were notified by my Corvette's message center that we had a tire that was going flat. I didn't realize at the time that I had special tires that allowed for continuation of driving with a flat, so I pulled off at a rest area when I discovered I had no spare tire and called for a tow truck. We waited an hour and a half after calling three different towing companies. It had begun raining. Finally, a tow truck arrived in the rainstorm. We loaded our vehicle onto the flatbed, and were taken the rest of the way home, which, by that point, we thought could not come fast enough.

However, during the time we were waiting for someone to rescue us, we became quite productive and made phone calls to various people who needed to be notified or provided with information as a result of Gabe's passing. This included talking with the funeral home, loved ones at home who were waiting on us for additional details, and others who we thought needed to be advised of the circumstances.

Since my wife and I both believe there are no accidents whatsoever, and Gabe has since confirmed this fact, the flat tire seemed fortunate in that it gave us some needed time to ourselves.

When we finally arrived home, Bill and Noah had already arrived and unloaded both vehicles. Bill had headed back to his house. We had only to unload many of the smaller items and mementos, taking them upstairs to Gabe's bedroom where we could sort them out at a later time. At that point, we had an entire home full of family which included Dawn's mother, her sister, Jill, and several of Dawn's nieces and nephews. It felt good to be surrounded by a loving family when we were so shaken and feeling so alone in what seemed like our big home, even though we'd always laughed that it was way too small when Gabriel was there. It's funny how things can change so suddenly and perceptions can change so quickly when something like this occurs. As I walked into Gabe's bedroom, my arms full of various items, I inhaled deeply to take in the lingering aroma of Gabe's body that still permeated the room. The realization now began to sink in that my wife and I had gone from a rather routine and normal lifestyle one day to an unimaginable and horrific tragedy the next, a tragedy that would forever change the balance and normalcy of our lives. It was a desperate attempt on my part to still have some piece of Gabe to hang on to and feel close to as I breathed in the fragrance of his former existence while standing in his bedroom.

All evening, thoughts continued to occupy my mind about how things would change, including what we would do with Gabe's music room upstairs where he spent so much of his free time mixing and producing music, to how we would preserve his bedroom — where I so badly wanted him to sleep again so that I could open the door once more so slightly, as I had hundreds of times before in his childhood, and look in on him with a smile in my heart and a feeling of satisfaction that all was safe and sound. Other thoughts, other questions crept in. Practical questions, such as how would we know where all of his friends were and where they could be reached when Gabe's friendships were so diverse and so segmented? So segmented, in fact, that one set of friends didn't even know that another set of friends existed. He had student peers, teachers, and middle-aged people who were his good friends, Hispanic and African-American friends, and so many other groups like musicians, and people at the record shops, on and on and on. If anyone showed him kindness or consideration at any time during his life, he befriended that person. It mattered not what the person's cultural or educational preferences might have been, for he only saw the best in each one of them. That's why they called him "a friend."

These were trivial matters to a degree that really had little significance at that moment. But Gabriel being gone had left such a void in my heart and mind that I felt compelled to pour over all of this and every minute detail of his life. It was a way of occupying my mind, of shutting out the pain to a degree, and to be productive in some small way. I wanted so badly to be able to turn back the hands of time...I would have gladly traded my life at that time for his .until I learned more...

While I'm thinking in those terms, my wife was experiencing a sense of physical loss to a degree that was nothing short of devastating to her. We will probably always suffer from the unimaginable physical and emotional loss, the shock of first seeing our son when we arrived at Saint Xavier University that night lying in a body bag in the ambulance, and the sense of wanting to correct the grievous error made when our son was taken from us. Still, this is our lesson to learn from. It's just so heartbreaking and penetratingly sad when it's viewed from a natural, mortal, parental perspective.

Even though we knew better and understood rationally that we could not change the past, it must be a primitive instinct that parents have when their child passes on to want to assume for the care of their child in every imaginable way again. And feeling that you still want the requirement of doing so even when you know that your child will no longer be present in physical form to hold, touch, comfort, direct, or guide, again.

I remember asking my wife, when we were all alone and about to go to bed, how she thought this would change our lives (as if I expected her to be able to enumerate all the different ways that we would be affected).

"In all ways," she replied, shrugging her shoulders. "Those that we are aware of and those that we aren't."

As we climbed into bed and began to feel at last some bit of physical relief from that exhausting day, we both began to cry again. We attempted to console each other, holding one another close through extreme emotional pain and mental suffering, the likes of which I have never known before. Indeed, I had never felt closer to my wife, however, than at that moment, as the tragedy of our son's loss had tapped into an entirely new depth of feeling that was greater than any we had come to know during the first twenty-one years of marriage.

Although I knew I had a busy day ahead of me, and despite my exhaustion, it was extremely hard for me to fall asleep. I tossed and turned, thinking over and over again about all the things I needed to do and about the responsibilities I had toward so many other people. It was as if my mind was making one mental checklist after another of all the details that needed to be handled; and through some subconscious kindness, and only then, could I allow myself to fall asleep. My wife went to sleep with tears rolling down her face, and I knew that our grieving process had only just begun. We were still in shock and it was just a matter of time before that shock wore off and the fact that our son was never coming home again would really sink in.

My wife and I both awakened early the following morning. We met our son, Noah, for breakfast and then traveled to the funeral home to discuss arrangements, hopeful that we would be able to view Gabe's body, this time without a body bag over him. The man who met with us seemed overly cheerful considering our sense of loss and grief. He twice avoided my wife's question, "Where can we view our son?" She was beginning to feel a good deal of hostility toward him, and it was obvious to me, that I needed to express her need for a direct answer. Immediately, the salesman responded:

"Well, he's not here," the man said at length, "but come right this way and we'll discuss this matter in just a few moments."

Finally, the man from the funeral home spoke those dreaded words that no one wanted to hear.

"He's not here," the man said, avoiding our gaze. "I'm not really sure where he is at this moment."

Our only desire was to see and touch Gabe again, and be as close as we could with him physically. My wife became so angry that I thought I was going to witness the first TKO ("technical knockout" in boxing terms) ever to occur in a funeral home.

During his long explanation of how the process works, I cut him off and asked him for a straight answer. He responded that he did not know where our son's body was, and that because Gabe's death had occurred out of state, there was no certainty as to how soon the body would be transported to Indiana. This infuriated my wife and my son Noah beyond words, but certainly by facial expressions.

"Well, how can we learn how fast this process will occur?" demanded Noah.

The man indicated that he would have to make some phone calls, which my wife felt should have been completed prior to ever meeting with us.

He gave us the name of the mortuary in Chicago where he thought the body may have been sent. We asked him if he knew anything about that mortuary.

"Not really," he responded, "but our network is a lot like FTD in that we have an existing group of people that we work with that we feel we can trust."

That answer set about as well with my wife, Dawn, as the previous remarks that he had spoken. She was furious that the funeral home did not have a better understanding of where our son was, especially in this hour of need when we so desperately longed to see him. I told the man to contact us as soon as he was certain of what the processes were and how quickly we could get Gabe's body back for viewing.

Later that evening, we received a call from the funeral director, who handled the remaining matter in a very responsive and professional way, explaining the process quickly and concisely. Noah went online and learned that the funeral home in Chicago that had picked the body up from the Chicago medical examiner's office happened to be one of the premier preparation and embalming services worldwide. This at least gave us some relief, although we were still anxious to see Gabe. Every effort, we were told, would be made to return Gabe by Tuesday (this was now Sunday), so that we could view him as early as Tuesday at 3:00 PM. Although we were not happy about this delay, we were grateful that someone could at last give us a time when we could finally expect to see him for certain, again.

The funeral director continued to communicate with us regularly and my wife was much more comfortable that all things were being handled as they should. While none of this disturbed me to any great extent, I respected the fact that my wife wanted complete knowledge of where our son's body was at all times. She needed to know who was touching or working on him, despite the fact that his spirit had already passed from the earth. She had always felt like the primary caregiver for him, handling all his needs from birth. She wasn't about to quit concerning herself with those things now.

The delay, it turned out, was due to a Cook County policy that requires that any corpse to be transported out of state from the coroner's office must first be moved to a local mortuary for preparation and embalming prior to being transported across state lines. These are union requirements. No one is exempt from this policy.

When Tuesday arrived, we went to where the body had been brought for final preparations. This included dressing Gabriel in the clothes that Dawn had carefully selected for him. For his final resting, she chose an outfit he customarily wore every day, including a beautiful multicolored sweater, gray cargo pants, which he dearly loved and wore all the time, and his favorite white socks which came out of my dresser whenever his were dirty or missing. Dawn also brought some hair wax that Gabe loved to use on his hair to make it stand up on end, giving it a "sleepy head" effect.

Finally, the moment came when we were taken back into a large room where our son lay motionless on a preparation gurney. As we approached his body, we could see the head of our son lying still, propped up a bit, his body now clothed in the things my wife had brought. Instantly, we all broke down and began to cry as we touched his hair, his face, his arm, his chest, any part of him that we could. We knew it was only the remains of his temple here on earth, but it was still our little boy, our son that we invested eighteen memorable, precious years with, loving and nurturing him, and watching him become such an extraordinary person.

Even with no makeup, for the funeral home in Indianapolis had all that they could do just to get him ready for us in time for the promised viewing of his body, Gabriel looked as beautiful to us as ever. Almost as if he were just sleeping, he lay silently, almost naturally in his final body form.

After we had been with our son for more than an hour, while the remainder of our family waited patiently outside to take their turn viewing Gabe, Noah turned to us and asked if we could step outside for a moment while he remained alone with Gabe. Probably due to the age difference of eleven years between Noah and Gabe, for the first time it appeared that Noah realized what their brotherhood had meant to his life and what it was going to mean to him now that Gabe was no longer with us physically.

As we stepped outside, we heard Noah burst into sobs, his emotions overcoming him in a way we had not heard since he was a little boy. Whatever his commitment was to Gabe during those few moments that Noah paid his respects privately to him, he became a different person from that time forward. Noah was still as loving as he always was, but he began coming around to visit and to see us much more than was customary. It was almost as if he had assumed both his role and Gabe's role with our family now. Gabe had always been very "family-oriented" and Noah had always been highly independent. So for many years after Noah went off to college and then moved into a career in advertising, Gabe's presence had permitted him the freedom of not needing to concern himself about who was caring for his parents' emotional needs and well-being daily. Today, it seems that his perspective is vastly different.

As our extended family and relatives walked in to view Gabe for the first time, tears and outbursts and echoes of sobs and grieving of all description broke loose as, one by one, each member of our entire family had the opportunity to see and to touch Gabe. It was almost as if they had to see him lying there cold as ice to believe that he had actually died. That night, Dawn and I talked much about his appearance on the gurney compared with his normal appearance when he was alive. We were struck that there really seemed to be such little difference in his appearance, and we were grateful for this.

About 9:00 that night, we were growing tired when Dawn asked me if I had any interest in talking to Gabriel.

I stood in stunned silence. Dawn's question echoed in my mind.

"Would you like to speak with Gabriel?"

Twenty years earlier, she had asked me a similar question about speaking with my grandfather, Elliott, who had been dead for several years at that time. There followed an incredible six months during which I was able, through Dawn's channeling, to speak with my deceased grandfather. Those conversations were detailed, compelling, rewarding, and spiritually so dynamic for me, that they were life-changing. I knew that Dawn had a special gift for this.

Dawn has been able to channel at various times while energies were strong enough, and she felt an urge or specific need to communicate messages or information to someone, but has always done so with the ultimate of consideration and reservation since that time that we spoke to Grandpa Elliott. She never liked revealing how intricate her conversations or thoughts with the afterlife spirits may have been. She always let others imagine that much of her thinking was due to her "intuition" for the most part. This way, no one was frightened or rejected her in any way. Acceptance for her is very important to her, and she has friendships everywhere she has ever lived or worked that speak to this.

However, she and I had not done this for almost twenty years. Nevertheless, I was so excited at the sheer thought of being able to speak to my son that I blurted out: "Yes! Do you think we can?"

She slowly responded with a look on her face that confirmed my greatest hopes at that moment. "Yes, I think we can."

In a way, this was such a bittersweet moment. A moment where the sadness, the suffering, the pain was overtaken by my joy about the possibility of being able to speak to my son again only days after he had passed from the earth. Oh, how could I be so fortunate to have this blessing at this time?

Gabe playing at his summertime condo time share unit in TN

*Grandpa Vaught, Second Cousin - Eric Michael, Gabe and
Dad during a vacation in Florida at an Army site*

CHAPTER FOUR

Communications from Gabe

As I sat quietly in our family room, my heart was pounding with anticipation while I waited for Dawn to let me know when we could begin our conversation. Two to three minutes passed. Reclining on our sofa, my wife placed her hands over her eyes to shield them from the lights and distractions of our family room, where the TV was on, as usual. I switched off all but one of the lights and turned the television down so that it would not cause any potential interruption. I asked my wife if she would mind if we recorded this and I had the presence of mind to find a recorder and a tape that was unused. She had no problems with the recording.

Lying there, Dawn surrounded herself with "white light" by giving a prayer (silently), a necessary step to prepare her mind and heart to receive the divine messages as distinctly as possible from the "spirit world" and to block out any interference from other forces. Then, almost on cue. our dogs began to bark. We have a Boston terrier named Butch, a black pug named Tinker, and a shih tzu named Blossom, who is aging and seldom moves much faster than a turtle these days. So when all three began barking at once, I knew something was causing a significant change in energy in the room.

Normally, the only time any of the dogs barked was when a visitor knocked on the door or when Tinker spotted a dog or other animal on TV that caused him to feel the need to defend our home from potential wild TV screen predators.

But this was different. A baseball game was on at the time. Instinctively, I knew that Gabe's presence had entered the room. As long as I live, I will never forget the moment when Dawn simply said, "Okay." This meant we were ready to talk. I knew that although I would communicate to Dawn, and in return, Dawn would communicate Gabe's words to me, if this was to be as it was so many years ago when we spoke to my grandfather, Dawn would recall very little if any of our conversation. She has to concentrate so hard just to pick up the energy vibrations and to understand or interpret the messages she receives that it virtually prevents her from recalling much of anything of any detailed description.

I didn't know what to say other than "Hi, son."

In return, I heard a soft voice emanate from Dawn: "Hi, Dad. I love you."

Tears welled up in my eyes. It was all that I could do to speak again as I choked on my own tears.

"Son," I said, wiping the tears from my cheeks, as a smile came across my face, "I am so thrilled and so happy to be able to speak to you tonight. Do you know what this means to us?"

And then there was a momentary pause. I really didn't know what to expect. I just waited for the response from Dawn.

"Dad, I am here with you now and I will remain here for some time," as Dawn related the words that Gabe spoke. "There is much to talk about and we will have many opportunities to do so in the days and weeks and months, and perhaps, years ahead. Today, I just want to tell you how sad I am for the grief that you and Mom are experiencing because of my passing. I can feel this, and I am here to comfort you. I know it's going to be a very difficult process for both of you. There will be many questions, some of which I will be able to answer, and some of which I will not. I'll do the best I can to try to answer your questions directly each time that we talk."

Wanting so badly to be able to speak at that moment, without hesitation, I interrupted him and asked: "Gabe, what happened? How did you die?"

At this point, we still didn't have any information on the cause of Gabriel's death, other than a determination that he died from complications of diabetes known as *ketoacidosis*, a condition that can cause death. Elevated blood glucose levels lead to a drastic rise in ketones, which eventually causes one to fall off to sleep, and without medical intervention, this results in multiple or massive organ failures.

After a moment, Gabriel responded: "Dad... what difference does it make how I died? It is far more important that you know the meaning behind my death, and what the future will hold as a result of this."

"Son," I said, "can you tell me how you died?"

"Yes," he responded. "Dad, I went to lie down to rest ... I had some tenderness in my stomach, and then suddenly, there was a rush of air and I became one with a large vacuum and just like that, I passed to the other side. It really seemed that it happened that fast."

"Dad," he went on after a pause, "it was so beautiful. I can't tell you what it is like here other than to tell you that if you can imagine the most beautiful day that you have ever spent on earth in your life and magnified that ten thousand times, perhaps you could imagine what it's like here. I am alone here now."

My heart sank at the thought of my son being there alone and by himself, though I listened intently as he continued.

"But don't worry, Dad, that's a good thing, not a bad thing. Being alone now is good because it gives me much time for reflection and clarification of what my purpose and intentions are here, as well as time for the learning processes that are necessary for the future.

"Dad, if you could see what I see you wouldn't believe it. I'm sitting on a mountainside looking down over a magnificent view of beautiful white trees that go on and on and on with a sky that is almost perfect. And, Dad, I am so happy now ....I am free of my diabetes, and I am free of all the illnesses and complications that I had throughout my life. I can literally fly, Dad. I have much to learn in the days ahead, but there is no sense of urgency because time has no meaning here. Unlike earth, where everything is measured by time, time is irrelevant here.

Dad, many times when spirits transition to this side, they have longer periods for recovery depending on how ill they were while on earth and how long their illness lasted while on earth. Because my transition was sudden and occurred so swiftly and I was young and relatively strong, I have my complete strength now. This is how I am able to have so much energy to project my communications with you."

At this point, it was all that I could do to take in what he was saying, while trying to contain the enthusiasm and the love and the emotions that I was feeling for my son as he spoke to us. While I listened to his words and the inflections of his voice, his language seemingly chosen so carefully, just as he did while on earth, these expressions I recognized as his and his alone. My heart and soul knew it too. This was truly my son speaking to me from the "spirit world," from the afterlife. It all flowed so easily from Dawn as she relayed his messages to me.

So many questions popped into my head that it was all I could do to keep from interrupting and asking Gabe to share as many new insights as possible with us. So, I vowed inwardly, then and there, to listen until he quit talking before I asked him anything else again.

When a pause of more than several seconds came, I knew this meant that I could say something to him.

"Gabriel," I said, "your mother and I love you so much. We would do anything if we could trade our lives for yours, and give back to you the life that you had here on earth."

"It could not happen that way," he said with conviction. *"My number was up, Dad."*

At that moment, I realized deep in my soul and with my conscious mind what he was telling me. Not only were we powerless to change anything about his circumstances, but *this was how it was meant to be.*

For, "All our plans for our life on earth are our choice and God's will," explained Gabe, "not someone else's." As he described it in greater detail, even before we come to earth, we decide upon the lessons that we need to learn and then we form agreements, with every single soul that we will encounter during our lifetime, agreements that govern what we shall learn and take from those encounters. When the time comes for us to leave, we must leave by the terms of the contract and agreements with all whom we formed our agreements with and were asked to be a part of our lifetime existence on earth.

Although I had some difficulty grasping the comprehensiveness of detail of this message that night, I sensed the reality of the truth that he spoke of (as though it seemed like I'd known this sub-consciously).

He went on to elaborate. "Dad, before I came to the earth, I entered into a contract with you and Mom and every single person who would come into my life, even those who were chance encounters. Our contract was the agreement of how long I would live, how I would live, what I would accomplish while I was on earth, what I would learn there, and what my purpose there was meant to mean to me and to others. When it was my time to go — and there was an exact date and time involved — there was no way for me to withdraw from that contract without sacrificing the fulfillment of my destiny. And, I would have affected the outcome of others' destinies. I could not allow you or anyone else to block the passage. It would not have completed me to do so."

Several other messages were delivered that first night. Some of which were very personal, and very private and so meaningful to my wife and myself. Some I simply placed less importance with because of my excitement during our exchange. However, the things I have just shared with you I cannot and shall never forget, because they were so powerful and because they showed me that my son was happy, at peace, safe, and where he belonged. That it was by his will, God's Will, and our prior agreements that we all entered into this life arrangement, despite the tragedy and grieving we still endure.

When Dawn awakened after having transmitted the messages from Gabe, she looked as though she had been asleep for hours. It took her awhile to come around to the point where she was consciously awake. She remembered some of Gabe's words, yet, as I had suspected, had a difficult time recalling much of the content of the communications. My wife explained to me (at some later time) that she is able to see in her mind different images and phrases and words at times that help her to conceptualize the meaning of the messages that Gabe chooses to convey to us. Sometimes, she said, it is just like reading a banner off of a computer screen. At other times, it is precariously difficult and she has to ask for repetition to comprehend the message from the spirit world. Depth of meditation, self-thoughtlessness, and perspective, all play a part in how easily the communications are heard by her.

Anxiously, I wanted to tell Dawn everything I could think about and interpret about our conversation with Gabe, which had lasted over an hour. Even though I could hardly contain my enthusiasm, I saw that it had exhausted her to communicate in this manner with our son. She said she would have to go to bed and that I would have to finish telling her the rest in the morning. So I respected her wishes and calmly laid my head down next to hers on the pillow, all the while thinking about how beautiful the experience had been and how fortunate and blessed I was to have two angels in my life — my wife, who cared so much that she used her greatest God-given gift to comfort me, and my son, who knew that both of them working together to comfort me during these most difficult hours of grief would make all the difference to my world. It has, and still does.

Morning came, and I could hardly contain my excitement. I jumped out of bed where Dawn was still sleeping and hastily into the shower, not even bothering to shave, throwing on my clothes, and heading out of the house after kissing Dawn good morning and goodbye for the day, all at once.

I suddenly had a renewed passion about what I wanted to accomplish and where I was going with my emotional, mental, and spiritual life. It seemed cathartic by virtue of the changes that had occurred within me in an instant the night before.

I was riding an all-time adrenaline high, that morning. Oh, there was plenty to do that day and details to attend to, including the cemetery requirements, the final funeral arrangements, and many other calls to make. Still, I can't even describe how high on life I was again, knowing that I was once more in touch with my son … albeit his living soul now.

My wife had cautioned me about talking to anyone about all this, for fear that not only was much of it very private and personal to us, but she couldn't be certain that she interpreted all the messages one hundred percent correctly (although it seemed to me that she had no difficulty making sense of any of the transmissions from Gabriel in our dialogue). After experiencing the same type of concern on her part some twenty years earlier when we spoke to Grandpa Elliott, I understood her desire to protect herself from any ridicule, or suspicions that she was losing it during this time of extreme grief for both of us.

I accepted her notion that some people would not handle this information well. Others might be put off by the idea that God would permit such communications. I had to be selective about the people I would confide in and take care in how I would inform them of my miraculous communications with my son! Still, how could anyone in my position contain this kind of information or excitement? Why would anyone want to contain it after experiencing this?

The first person I telephoned was Bill Green, my longtime friend and attorney. He met me in Dover, Indiana (halfway between Indianapolis and Crawfordsville, Indiana), and I played the tape for him of the recording of the conversation with Gabe. Bill listened intently to the recording and then, as if in a state of disbelief, he demanded more evidence.

"More evidence?" I exclaimed. "Hell, Bill, I can't even tell you how this is occurring, truthfully!"

Just like an attorney, I thought…never enough facts! Always demanding evidence, then more credibility of evidence!

Bill was excited though for me and for him. He worried that he was going to have me crying on his shoulder again and it had already been an emotional time for him too up to this point. He was relieved that something wonderful could come from something so sad.

We put our heads together and decided that, if this was a once-in-a-lifetime opportunity, then we were going to record a certain percentage of the communications, as would be permitted. Not only did I want to savor every moment, but we could share the experience with other people in the world; people who would become more aware and, perhaps, listen with an open mind, attempting to understand the importance of the messages and the communications. The importance to me was obvious, but, to some, the importance would lay in proving the existence of the afterlife consciousness theory argued by so many fundamentalists, scientists, and spiritualists throughout history.

On Thursday evening — the evening of the visitation service — after all the events were over, I went out for a drink with Dan Stenger, my childhood friend from the age of two, who is now an attorney in Washington, D.C. Dan had flown out that day to attend the funeral. Dawn and I are the godparents of Dan and Chun's two children, Emily and Caroline. Seated at a table in the bar, I described for him the communications that I had been having with Gabriel. Dan did not seem shocked at all. It was almost as if he had expected this type of communication as we talked about all the different concepts Gabriel had shared with me on that Tuesday night.

As I related some details from my conversation with Gabe, Dan noted how it all made sense in the context of Christian teachings, how Gabe's description of the afterlife and his ability to be present among us was consistent with Christian theology. He even spoke of how Gabe could, perhaps, help his own family at times. I knew that Gabe would love that opportunity as he cared so deeply for the Stengers.

Gabe sunning himself on the beach in beautiful St. Marten during a family vacation

and Dad sharing a special moment together in Washington D.C.

CHAPTER FIVE

Dealing with Grief while Taking in the Incredible Messages from Our Son

In the days that followed the burial and services for Gabe, we continued to receive communications from him that not only were spiritually uplifting and designed to comfort us to the degree possible, but which were also quite informative. At times, these messages have even allowed us to laugh again. Our son always knew how to help us do that so well! He has always had a great, though sometimes dry, sense of humor.

Our son made it known to us each time that we have spoken that he was and will be always with us, and that he could always respond to us and would like to do so as often as we felt comfortable in asking for him through our thoughts, prayers, and/or calls to him in spoken words. So although I communicated with him on my own for a while with mixed results — meaning that I felt that I was getting some of his messages, not certain of how many — I knew I needed to concentrate and practice much more to help the communications grow. (He confirmed that we were indeed carrying on conversations together and that I was receiving his messages very well by remaining open to his contact with me and believing in the process.)

Meanwhile, at other moments, I could sense that my impressions were coming with what I considered to be too many of my own thoughts and feelings. I felt that too much of my own personality was being mixed in with the inward dialogue to have total faith in the certainty of the accuracy of the direct communications between Gabe and me at all times. So, I decided early on, then, that it was best to let my wife, who was much more experienced at channeling, handle all further communications that involved Gabriel until I could be certain that I had learned how the process best serves us all, and I could learn to hear him more clearly by listening for him, and not simply to my own thoughts.

On all essential communications, I felt so much more satisfied that we were likely to receive clearer reception of the intended messages through Dawn. This meant that any time we were experiencing serious depression, or needed information of importance to reassure us of our sanity, or personally permit us to hear more about his world, we would use my wife's capabilities. The communications through her, trying as they may be to her physically, still seems so much more effortless, fluid, and easy to understand. Gabe's own unique way of expressing things is easily discernible when he speaks through her. I really enjoy this! It is truly like speaking to him in the flesh and has the affect of really impacting the messages even more.

He sometimes expresses frustration with me to a small degree (which I really enjoy, because it is so like his expressions in the physical world), and he also shares humor, laughing at my questions at times, which he perceives to be a bit off-the-wall, so to speak. I seldom prepare any rehearsed questions for him choosing, rather, just to go with the flow. Whatever we talk about is so beautiful to me. It inspires love, hope, and thanks for the blessings it creates for us.

"Son," I asked him on one occasion, "how do you think Jesus would feel if when I transition to your side, I simply followed him around for a while wherever he went?"

He did not immediately respond. But when he did he said, "I think he would be scared to death, Dad," and we both got a great laugh at that thought and expression!

We had many conversations in the days and weeks following Gabe's death, and several were not recorded initially. Some we did not record intentionally so that Dawn and Gabe and I could just have "private time" to ourselves. I'm not out to prove anything here as much as I am to record and report the truths as we are told them by Gabe and the others. This is important I am told, and that's enough for me.

Gabriel stated, that with this book, "we are prepared to be exposed and look forward to the increased communications between us all."

One day, while I was attending a Hispanic-Latino Forum business meeting at the Indianapolis Urban League, I met up with an acquaintance of mine, a beautiful, spiritual woman named Maria Pimental-Gannon, who was working on a local initiative project that we both had volunteered for. After we exchanged pleasantries, she asked me if she could speak to me personally about something.

"May I say something quite personal to you?" asked Maria in a serious tone.

"Certainly," I responded.

"I know that you are receiving communications from your son," she said, "and I think it's wonderful. However, I am getting information that I feel I should share with you. I fear that the communications will not always continue. Therefore, make the best use of them as you can, for as long as you can. And please understand that this is just to comfort you and help you through this difficult period when you and your wife are grieving so much."

I was taken aback by her kindness, her credibility as a holy person doing God's work, and for knowing the importance of that message to me. Irregardless from whom she received this information, I decided it didn't matter and that I should take her advice seriously. I realized at that moment that nothing really does last forever. So I began to take each and every communication as a precious gift and recorded many of them after getting both my son and my wife's permission each time.

Our conversations have covered a variety of subjects, including matters of religion — God, Jesus, Mohammad, Buddha; the nature of the universe; other galaxies; and infinity (though Gabe says it doesn't really exist); the different levels of ascension spiritually; angels and other spirits involvement with us in this world,; the transition from life on earth to life hereafter; the Bible; the Koran; everyday matters such as our favorite sports teams, the Chicago Bears and the Cubs; the destiny of animals; topography; telepathy; food; hell; Osama bin Laden; Gabe's friends on earth; my friends and acquaintances; my destiny; and his destiny. Gabe explained that he will not and cannot discuss certain things because of laws that govern his communications with me from the "spiritual realm." The subjects that are off-limits include:

- Anything that would provide to me or another person a strategic insight over something of relative importance, or regarding someone else in a given situation here on earth, that could change the course of my destiny or their destiny here on earth in any way.

- Lottery numbers and other such things that would change the financial fortunes for someone, changing the course of their destiny in a unplanned, harmful, or unknown way.

- Any type of personal or confidential information about another human being that would violate his or her right to their requested privacy.

- Any "holy messages" from his world that enlighten him about issues that are to be known only to those in the hereafter or place the greatest risk of confusion for others living here on earth without detailed explanation and further education of their importance to the future.

- Information that will or could do harm to anyone unless it is specifically for the purpose of preventing that harm as part of my own personal destiny or their personal destiny.

Gabe explained that he, along with all the "living spirits," are available to "enable understanding for those who care to know." They absolutely are not to prove any truths to anyone whether they are believers or nonbelievers, for each individual must choose between his or her own choices in fulfilling their own individual destiny. Enlightenment is a choice that we all can choose to have and to use, or to discard and discredit as meaningless to us.

My initial rule in talking with my son was to allow him to speak to us and then converse on whatever subjects he wanted to speak about during each session. As time went on, I discovered that he increasingly expected me to take the lead in the conversations, perhaps because he understood that I usually had more questions and wanted his access to the "higher understanding" as I called upon him. He continues, to this day, to increase his emphasis on not sharing the future specifically with me. He says that "the greatest experience and meaning that comes from all of living is in the self-discovery of new understanding."

I carry on a conversation with Gabe in much the same way as I would when he and I used to go for a drive or when we spent an afternoon together on a holiday just visiting and relaxing together. The difference is that my wife can not usually sustain the energy to complete the channel much beyond an hour and a half at any single sitting, and then she is so drained mentally. Because of this, I always hesitate to extend the channeling for fear that potential complications could creep in and cause interference, mixed messages, or a dark side to emerge in the channeling (which I have chosen not to go into at this time), as well as the probability that she would be exhausted unnecessarily, afterwards. I never wish to take advantage of my wife's gift simply to have the opportunity to communicate with my son. Her ability is a precious gift that should never be abused. So when she feels exhausted or simply not up to the task, we don't even try to communicate with Gabe or others.

Sometimes I would use my then-limited channeling skills to talk with Gabe, and much to my surprise, I have received good information many times that let me know that I, too, can and do speak directly with him if I only continue to practice listening, and not thinking. I must also concentrate on relaxing and allowing the thoughts to flow naturally from him more effectively through deeper focus on the absence of thought and God centered meditation.

Our conversations with Gabe continue to this day. Because many of the messages are not for everyone, and are highly personal, we have chosen to share excerpts of our communications throughout this book, both by way of transcriptions and through our personal interpretations. The voice quality of these recordings have not always seemed ideal, as we used a very inexpensive home recorder when we chose to record. The recordings were most commonly made in our family room, usually with dogs (playing beside us, barking, etc.), and a muted television that runs pretty much nonstop and on occasions turns itself to different channels or volume levels during our reading. On one occasion it turned from English audio to Spanish audio!

Securing my wife's permission to agree to the publication of our messages has been no small task. Due to her overwhelming grief with the loss of our son and her desire for privacy concerns, fear of ridicule, as well as the possibility of error through her interpretations of these messages, she has had, at times, a level of significant discomfort or concern with publicizing these extraordinary transmissions..

However, she became so good at receiving the transmissions that she was convinced beyond any doubt that these messages were God's way of granting us additional time with Gabe, on two different levels (planes) of existence. She also realizes that there are no accidents in this world and that the significance of sharing these messages of hope, enlightenment, and understanding, will far outweigh the personal level of concern for our own emotional issues with this.

Even though Dawn will never be certain that every transmission is completely one hundred percent accurate, and I doubt that it ever can be, we both believe that without a doubt, that we are speaking to and hearing from our son in each of his designed communications with us.

Dawn does not recall much from these conversations other than key expressions or facial changes that she sees Gabe make, such as, smiling, laughing, cringing, etc. She actually sees him aging and changing from a more physical form to more a spiritual form with each passing conversation now. But he lets her know that it is truly him each and every time that we communicate. And, our heartwarming and highly personal messages leave no doubt as to whom we are conversing with, as we require no further proof by evidence, as we have extraordinary faith that God and Gabe still have a desire to inform us of messages that will ease our pain and impact our lives in such a positive way.

Our faith grows and grows in God and His desire for our happiness. And, by my sharing this information with others, I know that I can grant the opportunity to those who are willing to view this without preconceived notions or harsh judgment, and that there are many things in our world that are misunderstood, misinterpreted, or mislead others in their thinking processes; some date back so far that dated organized religion, in various forms, must bear the responsibility for the indiscretions of misleading the masses at the time to prevent civil unrest, chaos, or coup attempts (conflict), to reform or change the leadership throughout history.

The church (in its prior form), demanded control over people's spiritual and mental worship practices. To rebel against those "old ways" and "customs," throughout the passing of time, often meant to disrespect (to some) the lives of those who brought us into this world. We then just accepted whatever notions were provided to us as our way of thinking and living, without questioning what we did not know or could not know at that time. And what we don't know as human beings is some exceptional quantum percentage of difference that is greater than what we do know and understand here.

In any event, Dawn has to be informed of the content of the messages after we have exited our communications with Gabe or others from the afterlife. It is all she can do to interpret, read, listen, and relay the information on a timely basis as it appears to her on the screen of her mind and through the depths of her mental awareness. Virtually all the communications with him come to her, as she describes it, through text and images that are shown to her at a specific spiritual transmission (ether frequency), and at different delivery speeds, as it were, making it difficult sometimes for her to communicate at a normal cadence. Therefore, sometimes the conversations you will hear on the recordings move along at a snail's pace, and at other times, the flow will seem fairly normal.

It is my desire that the recordings will ease your mind, allowing you to acknowledge the possibility that you, too, may be able to speak with your loved ones who await your belief and efforts to dialogue with them, if you so choose to communicate with them.

We were told by my son that millions of spirits try to communicate with their loved ones or friends each and every day, but, so few human beings listen and/or are willing to acknowledge that what they hear is what they believe they heard.

The fear of the uncertainty of how it occurs, why it is occurring, or what afterlife communication means to one's life can be difficult for so many, Gabe said. So people block it out or pretend that they did not truly hear anything, refusing to acknowledge the communications, and then, simply silencing their thoughts and refraining from sharing such communications with others, for fear that they will no longer be accepted as a "normal" human being.

Still, the communications are real and meant for individual and world enlightenment. Where do you think enlightenment through man's progress on earth comes from? (Certainly not man's own advanced self-education and wisdom.)

"Normal" does not actually exist! It's all so relative, Gabe has stated. What is "normal" for one person can seem to be "abnormal" to another. It's all in one's perspective, enlightenment, and awareness of what is important to them and what they choose to acknowledge in this life. We are all on different spiritual paths, and what one can embrace, another cannot. Enlightenment holds many opportunities, however, for growth. Growth can only occur when thought revision and applied understanding of heightened awareness is brought to our consciousness and considered above all previous thinking.

Communications with us can and does occur from those who have passed from earth, by our allowing ourselves the luxury of mental transitioning to a different realm of awareness and to a different frequency of thought and communication. It is within us all. But not all of us will ever comprehend or accept our ability to use our mind in this way.

Here are some of our communications with our son. These are transcriptions of actual recordings taken from some selected conversations from the afterlife communications with Gabe and other loved ones who came along. They are not shared to convert a single human being from one faith-based belief to another, or to change someone's life existence; they cannot do that. They can best serve as a great tool for hope and a factual reminder that we all have a choice of communications with loved ones or friends from the afterlife. There are people on earth that actually exist to teach others how to do this, and how to do it responsibly and safely. More importantly, though, the afterlife can teach us how to balance our perspectives and understand the truths that can guide our journeys home again (to the afterlife), while enhancing our quality of life here on earth during this experiential lesson learning education.

The spiritual afterlife exists to allow all spirits (here and hereafter) to continue to learn from their singular and mutual journeys, and so often, there is such profound understanding that results from their communications with us. For them, it is a way of "blessing" us through their life expression with us.

Mostly, they just love to be acknowledged and recognized as still being a part of our existence, and they want for us simply to acknowledge their existence for who they are now and our desire for them to be a part of our lives and to permit them to share in our physical/spiritual journeys here in the "teaching zone."

In essence, they help us to better recognize that we are never alone, never! We can rely on their love, their compassion, their sense of concern for us, and their guidance when asked for. Not to accept this is to deny the blessings that God gave to us through our recognition of our faith in Him and His creation of the afterlife. His creation of all things, and His reinforcement to us that nothing is impossible, are the greatest messages of hope that there is on earth. Without this acceptance, life seems to be mired in futility and hopelessness, all too often.

Everyday, in multiple ways, in so many literal and figurative ways for us to observe and experience here through our physical reality, God reminds us that we are surrounded by His love and the spiritual afterlife goodness and realities that also exist (though they are more often invisible to the senses of the human physical naked eye). It has been estimated that nearly sixty-seven percent of all human beings on earth believe in angels now. How can we believe in angels and not accept the fact that the "afterlife" exists?

With that hypothesis accepted, why wouldn't they want to communicate with us?

They (the afterlife spiritual world) live in and carry on in a different dimension that we cannot easily comprehend as human beings. But they see all and hear all that we as human beings do, particularly when we speak to them or simply think of them (they use telepathic capabilities) or pray to or for them. We are never alone in our journey! God intended it to be this way, so I've been told. We are all one in Him, and He is all one in and with us. We are not separate, even to the extent that we occupy the same space sometimes in His order of life.

Recorded conversation transcription:.

Gary: *Hi, Gabe*

Gabe: *Hi, Dad*

Gary: *We are going to record you tonight; is that okay with you?*

Gabe: *Sure, I don't care.*

Gary: *Gabe, do you know that it has been eight weeks today since you transitioned to the other side?*

Gabe: *It's been nine.*

Gary: *Okay, sorry. I just wanted to start out by asking you, what's it been like during these nine weeks for you?*

Gabe: *Well, I'm trying to be able to do more and more to affect the outcome of the things you could consider important, and I'm not able to do all that I'd like yet.*

Gary: *What kinds of things do you think we consider important?*

Gabe: *Learning for all those who aren't able to make themselves become more productive [inaudible].*

Gary: *You mean on earth?*

Gabe: *They are able to start to progress and then they stop, and start over, that's kind of like they are searching for the way.*

Gary: *I don't know why, but this last week I've been sadder than I have been the whole period of time. Do you have any idea why?*

Gabe: *[Inaudible] Well, I can't help but think you are trying to help yourself be more able to cope with life, although I can't help you as much as you need because it's a journey you have to make on your own.*

Gary: *It's okay. I wasn't asking for your help, I just wondered if you.*

Gabe: *It's in and out of grief; until you reach a point of saturation, then you'll be able to fall out of it forever.*

Gary: *Do you think that Mom's making good progress with her dealing with this grief?*

Gabe: *Mom will be able to cope every day. She'll want to help you make it through to.*

Gary: *I don't expect Mom to help me as much as I need to help her, but that's awfully nice of her to do that.*

Gabe: *Whenever you want to enable someone to make an adjustment in their attitude about grief, you find the words. It's an easy task for you. It's learning the words that's hard.*

Gary: *Well, what do you think about the progress I've made so far on the book? Am I doing a poor job by by doing it too quickly, or do you think I am doing the right thing by recording it quickly?*

Gabe: *Give yourself time to think about the purpose you have before you start to work each day. It will be better for you to complete a work you'll be proud of if you give it additional time to think about it before you start to type in the words.*

Gary: *Okay. How are Pam and all our relatives doing right now?*

Gabe: *I can see them from here. They are having a get-together, so at times that they are together, they are happiest, and it helps get everyone going to the places that they want to [inaudible].*

Gary: *You mean in their mind?*

Gabe: *Yes, through their mind they go, not physically so much.*

Gabe: *She thought it would be nice to come over and talk.*

Gary: *She [sister, Pam]wants to talk to me tonight?*

Gabe: *She's here if you want to talk.*

Gary: *I don't want to talk to her just yet, but I do in just a few minutes. But, I want to ask you a few more questions first. Tell her just to hold on for a second. Gabe, do you telepathically communicate where you are?*

Gabe: *That's what I'm doing right now.*

Gary: *But I mean do you telepathically communicate with the other spirits, or are you able to talk just like I do with Mother here on earth?*

Gabe: *I'm able to do either one. I can just look in someone's eyes and see what they want or need and I can give them reassurance by that. Sometimes I speak because it's good to hear voices for the people here. They can't get the same feelings with just receiving the information that they get when they talk.*

Gary: *Do you and Pam actually ever physically talk with one another?*

Gabe: *Sure, we laugh a lot, too. And it's so good to see others laugh. Because their whole faces laugh.*

Gary: *Is laughing just the same type of emotional response for you as here on earth?*

Gabe: *It's much more joyous here. No one cries a lot, or seems sad or moody. They are laughing through it more the same, not so [inaudible].*

Gary: *Why does Harry Caray cry when he sings sad songs then?*

Gabe: *He loves to sing. It makes him cry. He's not crying about his own sadness, he's crying about the sadness from the song. Like when you see a sad movie or hear a sad story that doesn't involve you.*

Gary: *Oh, I see. Do you enjoy singing, Gabriel, where you are now, or do you mostly just enjoy listening to the music?*

Gabe: *I'm not really able to sing that well. I keep hearing all the time what the music is. It's more like surrounding me.*

Gary: *Is it more like angelic-type music you listen to now?*

Gabe: *No, not at all like angelic music.*

Gary: *Is it alternative or hip hop?*

Gabe: *It's the music I always listen to. I can have any music I want. I just think about how I feel and listen for that music.*

Gary: *So you are able to produce through your thought process anything that you want? Is that right?*

Gabe: *Well, anything that I want to listen to.*

Gary: *Well let's say you decide to want to eat. I know you don't have to eat, but sometimes you do it for social reasons. Can you just imagine what you want for dinner, think about it and then it's there?*

Gabe: *Sure. That's the way it works here. No one can navigate their way through all the thoughts that occurred here so we just go with what we want. We don't have to justify any of these the things, so if we are hungry, we just eat.*

Gary: *Let's say you decide you want to see a movie? Can you just go see a movie?*

Gabe: *Well, right. We can produce a movie if we want.*

Gary: *In your mind, you mean?*

Gabe: *Or, by using our tools like we would on earth. It's not always the best to just blink and it's here. We like the activity of doing as well.*

Gary: *Do you have the physical sensation of touch in your dimension, Gabe?*

Gabe: *Yes.*

Gary: *So you can reach out and touch anybody you want, is that right?*

Gabe: *We can touch other spirits, other spirits or souls by either physically holding them or just mentally holding them.*

Gary: *Is it the same? Does it feel the same to be mentally or physically touched?*

Gabe: *Not exactly the same.*

Gary: *Which is better? Physical?*

Gabe: *For me?*

Gary: *Yes.*

Gabe: *I'd say that I prefer the physical touch still.*

Gary: *Okay, would people tell you they or spirits tell you that they enjoy the mental touch, right?*

Gabe: *Sure.*

Gary: *If people can produce whatever image they want of themselves whenever they want where you are, wouldn't everyone desire to be magnificently stunning?*

Gabe: *"Magnificently stunning?"*

Gary: *Sort of like an Elvis Presley on earth, for a man, or a Sharon Stone on earth for a woman?*

Gabe: *Where would we go to differentiate among each other if we were all the same? The beauty of being here allows us to be at our best. Whatever we feel that is. Typical beauty is only important when it's necessary to create what you need.*

Gary: *So physical beauty is very low on the priority list of things that spirits value where you are?*

Gabe: *Every spirit here is quite beautiful, and are all held in the highest esteem by one another so no one goes around saying this is more beautiful than something else.*

Gary: *I see. I see. So everyone there is respected equally.*

Gabe: *Yes, and there is no, not much competition in that form.*

Gary: *Is there competition for extraordinary mental capacity?*

Gabe: *Just like on earth, we admire those who develop the strength of the mind, but it's more admiration than competition.*

Gary: *Gabe, have you been helping or looking after Emily in Washington, D.C. at all?*

Gabe: *She's doing all right. She is being more like herself now. She ought to be happy about that.*

Gary: *So you haven't necessarily had to intervene and contribute to her in ways that would allow her to improve in her performance in anything?*

Gabe: *The world just got bigger because she wanted it to. I can just do some things to help her not do her work for her.*

Gary: *I see. Did you see her kick that goal to win that game over the weekend?*

Gabe: *That was pretty cool how she just changed her mind and then changed that result of the whole game. It became important to her to be the one who won that game. And I think she just decided to ask for the help.*

Gary: *We love those kids so much, Gabe. Anything you can do to help them would be appreciated, but I know you've got your own work to do as well.*

Gabe: *Dad, I can help now and then and I just think it's good to do that.*

Gary: *Gabe, I really want to excel at writing this book, and I don't want to take any chances of doing it poorly. If you have any other suggestions how I can improve as we go through this process; please let me know would you?*

Gabe: *Keep using the method that you are using and clearly translating. The information I give is hard and I'll keep trying to send it clearly.*

Gary: *Are you sending it to me while I'm thinking about what I'm saying in the recordings that I'm doing?*

Gabe: *The information is being relayed to you by me and by others here so you won't leave anything out.*

Gary: *I hope I haven't left anything out. I've thought about that today.*

Gabe: *Dad, just before you thought about it, so did we. And we decided to help you more.*

Gary: *My goal Gabe, is not only to write this book to educate people about all the things we've talked about — diabetes, the Savior, your work here on earth and hereafter, and the ability of human beings to be able to communicate with spirits if they like after they transition to the other side, and the messages of living in the spirit of Christ, and Glory be to God in all things, but it's also to be able to pass any other messages that come along as well. So I'll be listening to those, and I just don't want to leave anything out, Gabe. I want to give everyone and everything its due and I want this book to be such a successful book. I want it to be read by millions and millions of people. My dream and my goal is to have it sold into a movie and have the movie seen by millions of people so we can begin the process of teaching people to believe in the spirit of Christ and Glory to God in all things that we are discussing now that are real, and that they can do these things too.*

Gabe: *Okay.*

Gary: *I can see that you are not real enthusiastic about what I just said.*

Gabe: *Well, I just thought that we knew that already. It's not that I'm not enthusiastic.*

Gary: *I know, it's just that I have to remind myself, because I keep worrying that I won't be good enough or up to the task and maybe I'm the wrong person to put this thing, this responsibility, on my shoulders, and try to accomplish it. I just think that way sometimes.*

Gabe: *Worry keeps us away from our goals here, too. Just don't worry.*

Gary: *All right, be happy, right?*

Gabe: *Your control of your mind is not as good as it can be right now.*

Gary: *I know. What do you think I should do?*

Gabe: *Love makes us that way, and you are going to feel this until it stops. I can't believe you'll not be able to control yourself soon. It's like you lost all your life and you didn't.*

Gary: *No, but I lost my wonderful physical-bodied son, and so much of my dreams that were tied up in him.*

Gabe: *I know it's so hard for you to see that I'm just right here for you. I can't materialize; I just can't do that, but I'm going to try to show you more that I'm here.*

Gary: *Gabe, the other night at the Elvis Presley concert [movie] when I felt you and I heard you say, "Isn't this great Dad?" I just felt that. I mean it was almost like you were really there physically. It was that good of a feeling for me.*

Gabe: *Good.*

Gary: *We've got pizza coming. Do you want to help us eat it?*

Gabe: *Yes. It's good pizza.*

Gary: *Do you have anything like that where you are?*

Gabe: *I can have it. I can do the cooking for them like I used to at The Garrison. If any help is needed eating the pizza, I can do that too.*

Gary: *Well you are welcome to try. I don't know if there will be enough to go around, but help yourself. Hey, Gabe, one thing I want to ask you real quick — have you ever seen Penny's daughter since you transitioned to the other side?*

Gabe: *Lisa left the earth in so much pain that she's needing to rest now, you know, be quiet sort of until she gains more strength. She's really okay. She's just weakened and she'll have to continue to do work toward making herself stronger.*

Gary: *Any messages for Mammaw and Pappaw?*

Gabe: *Pam wants to say something.*

Gary: *Okay. Hi, Pam!*

Pam: *Hi, Gary, it's good to see you.*

Gary: *I love you, Sis, and I'm so glad you came over to talk to us. Thanks for waiting patiently.*

Pam: *Patiently? I wasn't patiently waiting.*

Gary: *What were you doing?*

Pam: *I was just twiddling my thumbs trying to get you to move along.*

Gary: *What do you want to talk to us about?*

Pam: *I have to say you're not able to put together a party like I had hoped. If you can't do it, just try to   ease off try to get this thing rolling.*

Gary: *What am I suppose to do?*

Pam: *At least get together with Donna and Kimmie and at least try to demonstrate to Mom and Dad how important they are to you all. Lance will help if you need him to. He is going to be able to take some time off and do whatever you need done.*

Gary: *What kind of party should we throw? I mean inviting all the relatives from Crawfordsville.*

Pam: *Keep it simple and short because they can't take a long, drawn-out process. I'd do some snacks and some cake with a topper on it that says "61" or something like that to let them know the importance of their life together.*

Gary: *Are you going to be there?*

Pam: *Of course, I'll be there to make sure it's done right.*

Gary: *I should just put you in charge.*

Pam: *I am in charge. I'm telling you, aren't I?*

Gary: *I guess that's true. I hadn't thought about it. That's the way it was when you were here and I   guess when you're there. You're still telling us how to do things.*

Pam: *Well, somebody's got to.*

Gary: *I love you, Sis, and I'm so glad we can talk to you. I miss you so much.*

Pam: *I love you, too, and I'm going to make it so easy for you to do this. To make contact with the ones I need to, to get them to help.*

Gary: *You mean with the party?*

Pam: *Yes.*

Gary: *Okay. This party is important to you, isn't it?*

Pam: *It's very important that we honor them.*

Gary: *Is this their last anniversary, Sis?*

Pam: *That's not my call.*

Gary: *How's Mom, doing by the way?*

Pam: *She's tough and she'll be able to beat this if she keeps on it.*

Gary: *Is it a bladder infection?*

Pam: *That's one of the problems.*

Gary: *What's the other problem?*

Pam: *I'll have to investigate more to find out because she's not willing to see it right now.*

Gary: *Is it the endoscopy that will help?*

Pam: *Endoscopy will rule out some things, but not really help.*

Gary: *How's Dad doing physically?*

Pam: *He's good for Dad. He's not ruling out coming here soon, but he's good in spirits right now.*

Gary: *Do you know how much he misses you and Gabe?*

Pam: *He does, and we miss him, too, but we hope he'll continue try to support Mom while she's not able to support herself.*

Gary: *Do you ever go back and sit and talk with Mom anymore?*

Pam: *All the time. And she's been able to comprehend it more since Gabe died. He's able to convince them of many things that I never could.*

Gary: *You're a good team, I'm sure.*

Pam: *He's my boy. He's here to help me.*

Gary: *Keep in touch with us, Pam. Is there anything you want me to pass on to Julie or Shelly?*

Pam: *Julie and Shelly are able to hear me too, sometimes. They can help you with the party.*

Gary: *All right. I'll call them and ask them to.*

Pam: *Me too.*

Gary: *Want me to tell Lance anything?*

Pam: *No. Lance has yet to come up with the courage it takes to believe in something so foreign to him. He'll be able to, just not yet.*

Gary: *Well say hi to Ronnie Reagan and all the others that you see there, Pam. Tell them how proud we are of them, and how much we miss all of our relatives. Just know, Pam, that you are welcome to come and talk with me any time you want.*

Pam: *Okay, hon. They're are all waiting for you, too, and will welcome any chance you give them to help.*

Gary: *I would love for any of them who could help us here to help us, and for any of them who would love to talk to us to talk to us. We welcome that.*

Pam: *Okay, hon. We've got to go.*

Gary: *Tell Gabe I want to talk to him a minute.*

Pam: *He's still here.*

Gary: *Gabe? Can you hear me, Gabe?*

Gabe: *What?*

Gary: *Thank you for letting me say a few words to Pam and I want to tell you how much I love you, son and I miss you very much right now, but I'm going to take your words and try to be more courageous, and go forward with my life. When the day comes that I transition to your side, let's hold each other and hold each other so that I can again embrace you the way I did when you were here on earth.*

Gabe: *Oh Dad, I'm so sorry that you aren't able to see me more. I'm still trying.*

Gary: *I'll keep trying too, Gabe. When I look at your pictures, it helps.*

Gabe: *What wonderful times we had, and we are going to have.*

Gary: *I believe you, son, and I love you so much. Do you have anything to say to Mom before we go?*

Dawn: *Okay, I got it.*

Gary: *I guess that means you don't want to share it with me? Is that right?*

Gabe: *Right.*

Gary: *I love you.*

Gabe: *I love you, too, Dad. Take care; I'm going now to see what is up.*

Gary: *Okay. Let's talk this weekend. Bye, son.*

Gabe: *Bye.*

END OF TAPE.

Tape 2

June 25, 2004

Gary: *Hi, Sweetheart*

Gabe: *Hi, Dad.*

Gary: *Can you believe, Gabe, that Butch sees you and starts barking? Let me ask you a couple of questions, Gabe. Did you know Penny was going to call tonight?*

Gabe: *She's really sad. She's suffering, suffering terribly. But Lisa's okay. She's gaining strength; she'll be able to talk to Penny soon.*

Gary: Oh good. That will make Penny feel good. What do you think about this Mr. Williams that we are seeing, Gabe? Did you go with us today?

Gabe: He's an interesting guy. He's so interested in what you are saying that he can't be too interested because he feels he wouldn't be doing his job.

Gary: You mean as a counselor?

Gabe: Yes, maybe he'll ask you some extra questions from time to time to help him see what you're talking about.

Gary: Gabe, were you surprised at the outcome of the Pacers - Detroit game?

Gabe: They're losers. [Referring to Pacers.]

Gary: [Laughs.]

Gabe: They can't help each other at all. They seem to be able to play until it's important, then they fall apart.

Gary: Why do you suppose that happens?

Gabe: I think they will be better next year because they need to have more experience.

Gary: Do you think they are going to trade anybody?

Gabe: Maybe Ron Artest

Gary: Who are they going to trade him to?

Gabe: The Mavericks.

Gary: Yeah, the Dallas Mavericks. That would be a good team to trade him to.

Gabe: Well, he'll be good for someone else.

Gary: What are you up to today? Are you still in class studying?

Gabe: *I studied all day for the main items on the agenda tomorrow.*

Gary: *Are you still in the class where you are studying the literal meaning of Jesus's words?*

Gabe: *Jesus's words came from the distant past. Now we're studying the not-so-distant past, when others tried to be wise like Jesus and they ordained themselves rather than allow God to do it.*

Gary: *Who is that?*

Gabe: *There are many of them. I think Mohammed was one. Israel still suffers because of all the practitioners of faith that really didn't know what it was about and put their own twist to it.*

Gary: *In your estimation, who should we be concerned about as a potentially evil human being on the face of the earth right now?*

Gabe: *There are so many that you can't begin to know them all. They have so many ways of being evil from the smallest to the largest capacities that can occur, so your job is to maintain your goodness because it counteracts them.*

Gary: *By having a certain number of people doing good things, it counteracts the bad things that they are doing?*

Gabe: *Yes, but they will double their efforts to keep the trouble brewing wherever they can. It's part of the balance of life to have evil, but it creates so much turmoil for the world.*

Gary: *Is God capable, Gabriel — if he so desires — to have the spirit world descend upon the earth and rid evil once and for all?*

Gabe: *That's a good story, but it will never happen because, the will of God is to keep balance in all things. So, if no evil would result in the world, because there would be less evil, more goodness would result in a terrible situation, too. The goodness would be diluted and would be in levels of goodness so that the bottom level of goodness would be evil. If you leave it alone to be balanced, it will be better and I believe it could contain itself that way.*

Gary: *So your mother and I just simply need to go on with our lives doing the things that will bring the most goodness to the earth? Is that right?*

Gabe: *All the people on earth have assignments to complete. Some are going to be bad people no matter what. Some are going to transcend all evil and be saints, but most are simply going to try to keep the balance between good and evil from overtaking their lives.*

Gary: *I see. How's Pappaw Vaught doing today?*

Gabe: *He's good. He's taking a nap.*

Gary: *Have you been checking in on him today?*

Gabe: *I'm with him a lot so he can get some relief from his suffering. I need him to keep trying to understand why this all occurred. He's trying, but it is so very hard for him since he loved me so much.*

Gary: *What about Mammaw Vaught? Is she okay?*

Gabe: *She'll be there for him when he has decided to go. She'll have to keep herself in good shape for this because she'll be so stricken when Pappaw goes.*

Gary: *Pappaw will go before Mammaw obviously, then?*

Gabe: *Pappaw has been the leader... always.*

Gary: *Yes, he has.*

Gabe: *Hey, Dad, keep trying to have the party for them.*

Gary: *You mean the anniversary party?*

Gabe: *Yes. It's important!*

Gary: *You mean it's going to be their last anniversary?*

Gabe: *It's a trying experience to handle all the details but you can do it and you'll be glad you did. There is work to be done by others, of course, but you'll be the one to orchestrate it all.*

Gary: *How's Noah doing, Gabe? We saw him last night and he was so happy on his birthday. About that camera, what a great idea that was.*

Gabe: *There are so few things that Noah wants, but he's already happened to find a use for the camera that he will enjoy. He's already taken a bunch of pictures. He's so proud to have it.*

Gary: *Thank you for that idea, Gabe.*

Gabe: *That's okay.*

Gary: *What kind of a monument do you want Mom and I to get for you? I know we talked about it at one time briefly. Does it matter?*

Gabe: *I kinda like the ones that have a lot of the words that mean so much to you on them. You can have it printed with anything you want. So be creative with it, but don't spend a bundle of money on it because it's a thing and not a person and you'll want to have some money left afterwards.*

Gary: *Does it appear that our financial situation is getting better, Gabe?*

Gabe: *No doubt about that. Getting better so you can have a better life without all the pressures.*

Gary: *I would have given it all up and everything I own Gabe — and you know this —for you.*

Gabe: *You can have it all though, now. And I'll prepare you to have anything more that you want. You'll have to be sure you want things before you can have them because they can overtake your thoughts if you aren't for sure of what you want.*

Gary: *Gabe, the only thing your Mom and I really want is in this world we know we are never going to have again...*

Side 2

Gabe: *It's going to be complicated but you need to follow up with all that?*

Gary: *Is your name on the title to that car? To your car?*

Gabe: *No. That's not what I'm talking about. I'm meaning the albums and music and the copyrights and the albums themselves that I made.*

Gary: *Because they are worth some money, is that what you mean?*

Gabe: *Well here's what I think. I think you'll know after the first sale of these albums what you've got. I can't remember exactly how much they are worth. It doesn't matter anyway. I'll keep in touch about that. I'll help to find the right people to buy them since I loved the music on them so much.*

Gary: *What about the copyrights for your music that you produced? Should I do anything with that?*

Gabe: *Go ahead and do it, although, it's unclear to me why you need to at this time. But it's fairly easy, so go ahead.*

Gary: *Did you know Russ offered to come over and help us with the albums?*

Gabe: *Russ said he's going to help you and he's going to buy some himself probably. He's so wise about music that he'll be a good source of information for you and a good friend to you too.*

Gary: *He would never take advantage of us though, right?*

Gabe: *No, he's an old soul, too, and he's got to have this direction for his life now to proceed any further. He won't take any chances on screwing that up.*

Gary: *Before I go tonight, Gabe, there is something I want to ask you. Can Blossom, Stinker, and Butch all see you when you are here talking with us?*

Gabe: *I hope so. I'll try to get their attention.*

Gary: *Why is Blossom barking?*

Gabe: *She's hungry.*

Gary: *So she just wants something to eat then?*

Gabe: *She's always so vocal about it, too.*

Gary: *Your mother and I love you so much and miss you. But we are so glad we can talk with you. It makes everything so much better.*

Gabe: *What if there were no boundaries to this? Can you imagine how it would be to see, touch, be with, and communicate with all the people that have passed on over here?*

Gary: *Of all time?*

Gabe: *Of all time. That's how I will be able to communicate from now on. It's amazing. And it's great to see the actions of all these people.*

Gary: *Is there any one spirit that you most respect other than, obviously, Jesus, or, a counterpart to Jesus?*

Gabe: *There are so many kind spirits here and there and it's almost impossible to come up with a name for you. It's like a piece of sand on a beach.*

Gary: *Wow! That's remarkable.*

Gabe: *Dad, there so many in any gathering.*

Gary: *In your dimension.*

Gabe: *Any gathering, whether it be here or there, have at least half of all its members with good spirits. The brave ones are the ones we have to help. They are deciding between good and evil and trying to make the decisions that will advance them more quickly. It's so hard for them, and we try so hard to keep them on track. But some will go the other way and have to learn again and again.*

Gary: *Gabe, Pappaw is so fearful that he might end up in hell. And, I have to think that that won't happen. But didn't you tell me that there really isn't a hell?*

Gabe: *There's no hell in Pappaw. He has to give up that belief. He's so good and kind that he'll be rejoicing for all time to be here.*

Gary: *I remember you told me once that there would be one hundred thousand spirits or more waiting to greet him.*

Gabe: *He's a good soul. And he's going to make a great being here as well.*

Gary: *Can you tell Mammaw anything about her life now or in the future?*

Gabe: *She has so many people she loves and she wants to help them all, all the time. Her name is "wonderful" to them. Her heart has no limits on what they can do. She has told me lately that she has to hold me close to her to feel my love again, and I try to be able to touch her with enough force that she feels it, but it's not easy to do that and I'm not sure she can feel me.*

Gary: *Do you think it helps to let her know that you are with her, Gabe?*

Gabe: *I think it would because she's so lonely for me and she's got some time before there's any way she can see me, so, I hope it will help to be there for her.*

Gary: *You are so kind and wonderful. Thank you, son, for thinking of all of us and for helping us and comforting us in our time of need. Thank you so much, sweetheart. We love you.*

Gabe: *You are so welcome, Dad. Be careful about the stairs when you go up and down at work. The timing of your step is off a bit. I can't say why, but you're going so fast sometimes it can cause a problem. Just be careful.*

Gary: *I just need to slow down at work?*

Gabe: *On the stairs.*

Gary: *I don't have any stairs at my work.*

Gabe: *Yes, you do. Outside.*

Gary: *Okay, son. I love you.*

Dawn: *Afterwards, he said the steps.*

Gary: *Okay. Good night. We'll talk to you soon. If you want to talk to us come to us anytime. I'm always open and I'm off for the next ten days. I'd love nothing more than to talk to you as much as we can.*

Gabe: *Go somewhere to be alone when you need to hear me and I'll do my best to be there.*

Gary: *Is the cemetery a good place?*

Gabe: *Well, while you are there, it can be.*

Dawn: *I'm not sure I got that right.*

Gabe: *While they can be.*

Dawn: *I've lost it.*

Gary: *Good night, Gabe. We are going to leave and go nighty-night now. But we'll be here to talk to you.*

END OF TAPE

Gary: Hi, Gabe.

Gabe: Hi, Dad.

Gary: *Hey, is it okay if we record this conversation so I can play it back for Bill, so that when we write our book, he'll be able to validate this and know that this as factual information we are getting?*

Gabe: *It's okay with me.*

Gary: *Okay. Gabe, how was your day today?*

Gabe: *It was a day like no other, Dad! There were many times I felt like I'd been born again.*

Gary: *Really?*

Gabe: *Yes, but not so much to the earth again. But I saw things so differently.*

Gary: *The television station changed. The channel changed. All by itself!*

Gary: *Stinker, come on, baby. I got your bone. Sorry about the interruption, Gabe. We don't know what happened there. That was quite unusual. The TV changed stations by itself and an alert came on at the same time. That has never happened before. Gabe, I'm sorry. What happened there? Do you know?*

Gabe: *No, not really.*

Gary: *Gabe, tell me about being born again. Was it unusual?*

Gabe: *Not really, just so much new information and it came to me all at once. It reminded me of being born.*

Gary: *Wow! Was it positive information?*

Gabe: *It was like being in a whole new world because of the altered shapes and colors available to me that are new to me in my thought dimension.*

Gary: *I forgot that colors are how you communicate now, aren't they?*

Gabe: *No, colors are a vibration of light. Because they vibrate so much more in this manner of being, the colors vibrate at a higher frequency causing more brilliance.*

Gary: *Wow!*

Gabe: *It was intensified today for learning purposes and it caused me to think about when the birth of a child occurs, the intensity of the light and colors it sees are so much greater than those it's seen before. It's fascinating to see the world in that way and I wonder why it came to me today of all days.*

Gary: *Is there something unusual or special about today?*

Gabe: *It wasn't anything I can point to that made it different. Just learning a new thing makes it different.*

Gary: *Gabe, I'm sorry I don't know why Blossom is over here barking, but she's looking at the hallway and barking for some unknown reason.*

Gabe: *Probably the cat.*

Gary: *Oh, that's probably true. Well, Gabe, would you say that this was the most educational day you've had?*

Gabe: *When I think about it, it could have been. It's because the unit of time is so short and the experience so great within it that I think it was the most intense learning time.*

Gary: *Wow! Does the intensity of learning get bigger and better for you each day that you are on your side?*

Gabe: *I'm more receptive to it, I believe, and it seems like that, but it could be my lack of experience here yet. I don't know.*

Gary: *Are you learning with other spirits at the same time, or is this just an individual educational journey that you are taking?*

Gabe: *I'm with other spirits any time I wish to be and I can see them all the time if I chose to. But I need solitude from time to time.*

Gary: *So is it that easy that you can just blank out everything else and concentrate strictly on what you are trying to learn if you choose to?*

Gabe: *Yes, it's very easy and it's necessary for me. It's intense learning, not easy learning. Mostly it's because I can't hang onto the moment long enough to absorb it all without solitude.*

Gary: *Are you expected to absorb it all?*

Gabe: *No expectations and no grades or anything like that. It's all about me and my spiritual journey. No one grades or justifies or prejudges my work here.*

Gary: *Have you ever had a day — or let me say this, a relative experience over a relative period of time — where you didn't comprehend everything? Would that be okay, because you could go back and try again?*

Gabe: *Yes, but the moment passes quickly and I'll do whatever I can to grab it then rather than wait until the next opportunity. I'm still in the "earth mode" somewhat, meaning, I feel the need to accomplish a lot quickly. It's not necessary; it's just me trying to adjust here.*

Gary: *Sure. Would it be fair to say that you're still working with a level of sense of urgency when there really isn't any sense of urgency on your plane? I'm sorry, on your dimension?*

Gabe: *The sense of urgency exists within me, not outside me so much. While you were waiting to see me here, I can be many times away from you and back.*

Gary: *Doing things that are productive for you, right?*

Gabe: *Or, just things I want to do.*

Gary: *Do you have time just to do nothing, Gabe?*

Gabe: *Just "nothing" doesn't really exist, even there. Remember "nothing" is something because it means rest or inactivity or reveling in sunlight and just relaxing your mind to absorb more later. So, if you mean what I think you mean, no, everything has a purpose. But it's the same there, if you think about it.*

Gary: *I didn't mean "nothing" literally, I meant "nothing" figuratively. In other words, do you just have downtime where you don't have to do anything, to accomplish anything?*

Gabe: *As one likes it, that's how it is, so if I want time to reflect or just rest, I can. My needs are different now as sleep is not a priority.*

Gary: *Do you have time to sleep?*

Gabe: *Sleep is a way of resting and I need to rest still, so I do sometimes…it's just my desire. [Barking]. Butch can't deal with me this way. He thinks he can still get me to do what he wants.*

Gary: *Does he see you? Is that what you are saying?*

Gabe: *He senses me more than he sees me. He knows I'm here somehow, but not like I used to be.*

Gary: *So, in other words, he can sense you, but he doesn't have to see you to know that you're here.*

Gabe: *Right. He's never needed to see to know I'm around..*

Gary: *Can I have this time with Gabe, please? [Barking continues]*

Gabe: *I think he said "no," Dad.*

Gary: *[Laughing] Can you actually tell what he is saying?*

Gabe: *No. He's a dog.*

Gary: *I know. Are there dogs where you are, Gabe?*

Gabe: *Everywhere.*

Gary: *Do they do the same things they do here on earth?*

Gabe: *They run around and bark and play. They do dog things.*

Gary: *Is it the same with all animals? I mean, do you have like cats, birds, and things like that?*

Gabe: *All animals, but they get along better here because there is no need to eat so they lose the preying instinct and keep better company with one another.*

Gary: *But they cannot be of any harm to you in any way?*

Gabe: *No way. I don't even think about them harming me.*

Gary: *Gabe, what is the most beautiful thing about where you are in your estimation? Is it the white, the vibration, the other spirits? What seems to be the most beautiful aspect of where you are? Or are there just so many things?*

Gabe: *Some of the things I enjoy are the water is like silk, sort of. Here, you don't realize that when the vibration of water molecules change, it becomes more silk-like, rather than wet. I don't think that's a good way to put it, but it seems appropriate in a way.*

Gary: *Is there oxygen required where you are, Gabe?*

Gabe: *No. But it's here and our souls shimmer when we vibrate so much. The wind and water elements are the same, but appear different because of the vibrational change.*

Gary: *Gabe, would you say that the differences between where you are and earth are dramatic, or are they just minute if you compare item for item?*

Gabe: *Well, they have to be different, or you would see parallel universes and that would be so confusing. So it appears different and there are a lot of differences. So everything is lighter and more pliable and removed from your reality.*

Gary: *Do you have buildings and things like that?*

Gabe: *Sure. The akashic records are in a building that is magnificent and full of light crystalline qualities that are translucent almost, but not quite. You can't see through them but the quality is kind of like, uh, I don't know, like a translucent, extremely thick piece of glass, but yet you know it's some type of stone.*

Gary: *Is crystal revered where you are, Gabe?*

Gabe: *Crystal [TV sounds very loud without being turned on and then goes off] is like limestone is to you. It has a lighter, more shimmering appearance and it feels substantial, but unlike stone. I don't know how else to tell you about it. It's not revered anymore than building materials there are revered.*

Gary: *Do you have all your senses, Gabe? Can you hear, see, smell, touch, and that type of thing?*

Gabe: *Sure. Why wouldn't we be able to?*

Gary: *I don't know. I just thought I would ask.*

Gabe: *I have more than I did… not less.*

Gary: *What additional senses do you have?*

Gabe: *Sensation of being in the presence of others is much stronger here, so you don't even have to look around to see who is there. You know by their presence who it is.*

Gary: *You mean, you know every spirit there who is on the other side?*

Gabe: *I know them like they are in spirit, not like friends or anything. Like you would know people are people, not necessarily your friends.*

Gary: *In other words, if you sensed someone was nearby, you would know who that someone is in spirit form?*

Gabe: *I would know they are spirit, not who they are.*

Gary: *Oh, in other words…oh, I see. I thought that you meant you knew their names and that type of thing.*

Gabe: *Only if they want me to and then they can give me whatever they want me to know so I can become familiar with their attributes and soul wishes.*

Gary: *Let me use this as an example. Do you remember Abraham Lincoln, of course?*

Gabe: *Dad…*

Gary: *I'm just using this as an example.*

Gabe: *I did study!*

Gary: *[Laughing] Gabe, what I'm getting at is, if Abraham Lincoln is in the spirit form, would he want to be identified or have people know who he is, in spirit form?*

Gabe: *Abraham Lincoln could be here in spirit form and if I wanted to, I could approach him and see into what he wanted me to know, but he's not available to be my friend or anything. He's got his own world of souls and personalities that he hangs out with and chooses to be with.*

Gary: *[Barking and growling] Butch, Please! So in other words unless every spirit wants to share with you what they are all about or who they were previously —?*

Gabe: *I've never come upon one who refused to acknowledge who they are. It's not like earth, where everyone is so guarded. Because there's no danger, so you could see anyone here and know that you're protected from evil types of influences. They just don't come to us here.*

Gary: *Where do evil influences go? Do they have their own plane of existence or dimension of existence?*

Gabe: *I believe the evil we refer to on earth is not really what we thought. It's a complicated form of teaching that seems barbaric* *in retrospect. They all have to exist there in order to achieve balance and harmony within the natural influences. There can't be learning where there isn't evil or whatever you want to call it..*

Gary: *We call it evil because we don't know what else to refer to it, is that right?*

Gabe: *Evil has become a popular way of stating what we don't like. In some instances, it's good to one group and evil to another, so it's all relative to perspective.*

Gary: *I've never asked you; what's on the sixth level?*

Gabe: *The sixth level [inaudible] is amalgamated with the righteous of the fifth level. In other words, it's unknown to me exactly what occurs there because I haven't achieved it yet, but all levels are the pure essence of the previous level. So, the excess drops away.*

Gary: *So when you reach level seven that you said you would aspire to, that's where you get to molecularization?*

Gabe: *What? The seventh level is the same way as the sixth, and the fifth and the fourth: it is just the essence of the previous levels.*

Gary: *So there is no such thing as molecularization on the seventh level?*

Gabe: *Associated with some of the changes from level to level, but remember energy is not always molecular. It can become even more distended than that.*

Gary: *More what?*

Gabe: *Distended, but scientific explanation is not available to you, Dad, because you are there.*

Gary: *Because we're not enlightened enough, right?*

Gabe: *Well, yes.*

Gary: *Gabe, I'm assuming that since you can see a great deal more of the future and the present and perhaps even the past, you have to be more knowledgeable than we are.*

Gabe: *The future, the past, and the present are all contained with each soul. It has no meaning to remember the past or predict the future because each second (or even nanosecond) is all you can experience at that time. So, past and future are wound into a conglomeration of facts and don't need to be disseminated, because they are of no use.*

Gary: *So where you're at, you told me yesterday that can see my future clearly because I allow you to read my thoughts, but all you are really reading is my higher consciousness. Is that correct?*

Gabe: *The future is here, and that's what I meant when I said your future. It's not the day-to-day you need to be concerned with. It's the higher level of thinking that is required here.*

Gary: *So I need to stay here on earth until I can raise my level of thinking to prepare myself to leave. Is that right?*

Gabe: *The willingness to learn about the higher levels will help you to transition easily and without fear, but so much can only be learned here, because that's the purpose of the transition. The lessons there are only there and are only available to you there, and your enlightenment here cannot be achieved on earth. It's impossible or you would already know the answers and no learning could occur.*

Gary: *So, we are learning on two different levels. We are learning on earth by experiences that we have. How are you learning where you are?*

Gabe: *Knowledge comes to me through the souls who are here only to assist me in the knowledge and preparation, so if you could remember everything from here to there, you would already know that it so short term there. The knowledge you must pick up there is essential because it's important to know the physical requirements and how they integrate with the emotional and* *mental expectations that will occur. Everything physical needs to be learned elsewhere, not here.*

Gary: *Is ours strictly a teaching zone?*

Gabe: *No. Some learn more about the emotional side while being there and some more about the physical and some nothing at all.*

Gary: *You mean some people come here and never learn anything?*

Gabe: *Don't learn anything that they didn't already know. It's unfortunate because it's wasted time and you don't encourage your soul to learn and some can't.*

Gary: *Is it true that the higher level of handicap you have on earth takes you through a higher level of ascension when you transition over to the other side?*

Gabe: *The handicap you choose will be the one that allows you to learn necessary skills for later. It could be karmic so that you experience what you inflicted upon another. It can have nothing to do with karma.*

Gary: *Gabe, one last question that I have. [TV blurts out a tornado warning.] Is a physical handicap of diabetes a lesson that I am to learn here on earth? And if so, what would it teach me when I transition to the other side?*

Gabe: *Diabetes has always been the way of teaching some people the meaning of self-discipline and the lack thereof. That's why it moves so slowly when you take the caution of being diligent with your care and moves quickly when you don't.*

Gary: *So it has nothing to do with feeling loved or any of those psychological and emotional possibilities?*

Gabe: *It's not a psychological disease. It's a disease that requires much diligence and types of patience. The disease can be a haven for those who wish to become more tolerant and cognizant of pain. Sometimes, people have it simply because the body breaks down* *earlier than planned or with the normal rate of aging. It's not always a karmic duty. Sometimes it's the way out of life, but for you, it's the way you chose to be more structured within yourself and more tolerant of my needs because you knew that the likelihood was that we would tolerate each other better if we had a common ground to walk with one another on. The main reason you have become so careful with your disease is my disease required you to be the person who taught and trained me and in doing so, it required you to take care of yourself and therefore, lengthened your own life. The way of disease is often a tough way to learn a lesson needed for growth and it takes its toll on belief sometimes, that the way of the Lord is wrong. No way of life is wrong. It's only harder or easier than another.*

Gary: *Gabe, I want to tell you that I don't feel handicapped even though I have my days when I don't feel well and therefore, if I chose this handicap for any reason whatsoever that I don't understand now, I've accepted it. I will continue to work at trying to do my best to minimize what effects it has on me, but I do recognize that it is a chronic illness and therefore it's very dangerous.*

Gabe: *Your attachment to the disease is lengthy. It's been with you several times and you can handle it pretty well now. You may want to choose another disease next time because it is not contributing as much to your growth as it could.*

Gary: *Gabe, why do we have to choose diseases at all?*

Gabe: *You chose it because you chose it. It's not really happening anyway. You know that whole illusion idea is really true.*

Gary: *You mean I don't really have diabetes?*

Gabe: *Not really. You won't know much meaning of illusion until you get here. Everything that you need to know about your life is tied to the illusions that you created to learn.*

Gary: *I see. You don't have illusions where you are?*

Gabe: *Illusions aren't really needed because we have all knowledge we need. Creation of illusions assist in the experience of learning for earthly lessons, like disease.*

Gary: *Gabey, I love you so much. I know you know how proud I am of you again. And thank you for taking this much time to visit with me tonight.*

Gabe: *Hey, Dad?*

Gary: *Yes, son?*

Gabe: *It will be awhile before your kindnesses all start to believe that they are producing the results you need and want, but every time you try to become more loving and caring, it helps to move you forward. I know you were there for me and you were there for Mom, so keep trying to offer your genuineness.*

Gary: *Why is it so funny when I try to be so genuine about the things that I do? I don't understand.*

Gabe: *Because it's so easy to be genuine, you try so hard. It's kinda cool to see you being so perfect and everything.*

Gary: *I try to put my heart into everything I do now, son. I don't always succeed, but I try.*

Gabe: *I know that you try and that's all it's about anyway.*

Gary: *Thank you so much for talking to us so long tonight, son, and tell Pam and Uncle Wilson and all my uncles how much I love them.*

Gabe: *Yes, when they come here tonight, I'll be the one to tell them and move them along the way. Everyone has the love you want to express because they get it from you when think about the times you had with them. Even Pam can remember when you were so young and you loved her so much. The feelings transfer so easily here.*

Gary: *That's a lot of information tonight. Thanks again, sweetheart. I want to tell you that whenever you want to come to me, go ahead and come to me. I'm always available to talk.*

Gabe: *Love you, Dad, and I'll be there for you if you need me.*

Gary: *Gabe, do you want to tell Mom anything before you go?*

Gabe: *Well, when we talk, the message comes to you before it comes to the others and I'll be coming from the heart as well. Mom's heart was going so hard at the grief today that she will be tired for several days over it. It's becoming better, but it's hard to watch. Mom and I have been touched with each other's love here, today even, so keep trying to be calm and rational while this cycle completes itself.*

Gary: *I will, son. I love you so much.*

Gabe: *Are you ready to go, Dad?*

Gary: *I'm not ready to go, but I'm worried about Mom being so tired.*

Gabe: *Time to go, Dad. I'll be back and I'll bring some friends, just like I always do.*

Gary: *Great. I love you and I'll talk to you soon.*

Gabe: *See you later, Dad.*

Gary: *Good night, sweetheart.*

END OF TAPE

Gary: *Is that you, Gabe?*

Gabe: *It's me.*

Gary: *Did we wake you up?*

Gabe: *No.*

Gary: *Did we take you away from something?*

Gabe: *No.*

Gary: *Well, it took Mom a while to communicate with you tonight so I thought there maybe there was something going on.*

Gabe: *Nope.*

Gary: *Do you want to talk to us tonight?*

Gabe: *Sure.*

Gary: *You don't sound very excited. I thought you'd be excited to hear from us after not talking for a couple of days.*

Gabe: *Well, I hear from you anyway whenever you talk with me.*

Gary: *Oh, okay. Is this by any chance getting old to you, Gabe?*

Gabe: *No way. It's just that I can't be here on time always.*

Gary: *Well I understand. But I don't want to take you away from other things. Remember us talking about that?*

Gabe: *I'm here for you right now. So don't worry, Dad. It's okay.*

Gary: *What did you do today?*

Gabe: *I've been away most of the day to see why the "Way of the Cross" has been forgotten.*

Gary: *The "Way of the Cross?"*

Gabe: *Yes.*

Gary: *You mean the cross that Jesus was sacrificed on?*

Gabe: *The "Way of the Cross" is a crucial part of training that some may need to be reinstructed in so I came here today to enable that to happen.*

Gary: *Can you tell me something about the basic principle of the "Way of the Cross?"*

Gabe: *Usually, I have to be careful about what I say about the holy things that are being taught here. It can take away from my experience to discuss it fully before you arrive here. Never mind...I can't take the time to tell you because it's a lengthy process.*

Gary: *Gabe, the other night when we last spoke with you, you said you were on your way to the World Savings Bank. Was that in Arizona?*

Gabe: *The World Savings Bank has a structural issue to take care of that recommended we place our names on a list of people who were going to have a process of delivering news to those who would be affected. It's a difficult cause to be involved with right now.*

Gary: *Is it a financial structure? Is that what you are talking about?*

Gabe: *It is a financial structure.*

Gary: *And it's probably affected by their poor investments made through companies that had corporate fraud?*

Gabe: *All I know is that the people most affected are not at fault. The ones who have caused it cleared out long ago and left the personnel to reap the poor investment advice.*

Gary: *What happens to people like that, Gabe, that take money selfishly and fraudulently at times?*

Gabe: *They tend to have a great deal of trouble with all things in their life and the underlying cause of greed is fear and it intercepts all the good that could have come their way.*

Gary: *So, it's two different energy forces that collide and the negative energy from the fear prevents the positive energy from the opportunities that might have come their way from ever reaching fruition, is that right?*

Gabe: *You have answered your own question. It's kind of like that, only a little more complicated when you consider all the forces that work in this situation.*

Gary: *Gabe, outside of God's energy, what is the greatest single energy known to the spirit world?*

Gabe: *All energy is equally potent to all of us. It's as if the sum total of all energy was distributed by the universal power to each individual soul. It's activated when needed then placed away when not needed, so, therefore, all souls have basically the same energy amount.*

Gary: *But I meant like, not just energy from some of us, or discovered through human beings or spirits, but about the energy from the sun or energy from the planets, or energy from radiation, things like that?*

Gabe: *I'm not really tuned in to what you are asking, Dad. I can't tell which form of energy would be greatest. It would depend upon the force of the action that was required to develop the energy.*

Gary: *Okay. What has been the most enjoyable learning process, or learning lesson, or learning enlightenment that you have come across since you've been on the other side, Gabe?*

Gabe: *I've been searching for the most enlightening thing that I could possibly learn. I can't be sure which it is yet, but I have enjoyed the process of learning to communicate through glance and through non-verbal types of communication with other souls who are learning it as well. It is so much easier to use your image area rather than your mouth to form words much of the time. By the way we say things, we injure others, not meaning to, while imagery is more precise.*

Gary: *Gabe, when Einstein was living — by the way, is Einstein on level four?*

Gabe: *I don't know. I can't see.*

Gary: *Who can't see?*

Gabe: *I can't see if he's here or not.*

Gary: *And you've not thought to look for Albert Einstein?*

Gabe: *He's not been here with me at all.*

Gary: *Could you find him if he was there?*

Gabe: *I suppose. Why would I though?*

Gary: *'Cause I wanted to verify something. Supposedly at some point during his life on earth, he explained to some people that he felt he was using approximately seven percent of his total mental capacity and that the average human being uses somewhere between three percent and five percent. What would you say you are using where you are?*

Gabe: *I believe that he meant he was only using seven percent of his brain capacity. We don't depend upon our physical brain any longer, so it's not the same equation.*

Gary: *So, do you have mental capacity?*

Gabe: *I guess so because I'm still able to talk with you. So I couldn't do that if I didn't have any mental capacity.*

Gary: *Well, I understand the essential fundamental aspect of what you are saying. However, my point is, didn't you tell me that there are spirits that even though you appear translucent, appear to have physical image in your dimension?*

Gabe: *Sure.*

Gary: *Then wouldn't they appear to have a mind or a head?*

Gabe: *They have physical imagery. They can have a head, feet, hands to hold things, but we are not run by a physical brain.*

Gary: *What are you run by then?*

Gabe: *Mental energy.*

Gary: *Am I asking too many questions or can you answer these kinds of questions?*

Gabe: *I can answer them to my knowledge level.*

Gary: *Okay. Where does the mental energy emanate from in your energy field?*

Gabe: *It exists always. It exists in your physical body as well. It's what you know as the soul. You can have knowledge of your soul any time, and you do. So, it's that energy that propels us out from the physical body and into this realm ruled by energy.*

Gary: *Would it be a fair assumption that our souls are what we refer to as our higher levels of consciousness?*

Gabe: *Our souls have a higher level of consciousness, but the higher level of consciousness is not all there is.*

Gary: *What else is there?*

Gabe: *There are many parts of our existence labeled as energy force; mental energy, social energy, higher consciousness, and there are spaces within our energy diagram that were created by God or the universal mind that have no name that I am aware of that permeate our beings with a type of love energy. In other words, the empty spaces are not really empty. They are filled with this love energy that perpetuates the life of our soul.*

Gary: *So love is the greatest force that there is. Is that what you are saying?*

Gabe: *Love energy is the largest amount of force, but it can't be corralled so it can be freely distributed everywhere.*

Gary: *Does it exist in all of space, including infinity?*

Gabe: *Well, infinity doesn't exist, but it permeates our world and yours.*

Gary: *Why do you say infinity doesn't exist?*

Gabe: *Infinity, by definition, does not exist. No, it can't get to infinity. It is a description of that whichdoes not exist.*

Gary: *But didn't you tell me once upon a time earlier in our conversations that you know no limits or no boundaries to the space-time continuum?*

Gabe: *Yes.*

Gary: *So what would that be called then?*

Gabe: *Well, yeah, it could be, or you can call it whatever you want. It simply exists. It doesn't require a name or a word to describe it, because it is.*

Gary: *What is the most remarkable earthly feat that you have witnessed since you transitioned to the other side?*

Gabe: *You mean the feat that required the most energy?*

Gary: *Yes.*

Gabe: *That's hard to say. There are so many types of energy. It's unbelievable what it can do; every day, people are healed that couldn't be healed. Crazy things happen that are about to not happen. The way of the world can be changed by the action of one bit of perpetual energy and I couldn't really narrow it down because it's like picking one most beautiful flower out of a world full of flowers. It can't be done really.*

Gary: *All right. Let me ask you your opinion on this. Since you've transitioned to the other side, what have you seen on earth that troubles you the most?*

Gabe: *Within my own narrow scope, I see hopelessness among the very youngest members of our family and that troubles me most.*

Gary: *You mean our personal family, or the world's family?*

Gabe: *Our family.*

Gary: *May I ask who those people are?*

Gabe: *Littlest ones are the most affected by the lack of hope in the future.*

Gary: *On both sides? On my side of the family as well as your mother's side?*

Gabe: *Well, I am able to see everyone in both sides of your family and Mom's family and there are thousands of them.*

Gary: *Thousands of living people or thousands of spirits?*

Gabe: *Thousands of living people. Your family is not just your brothers and sisters. They come from everywhere. You are related to so many people but when I see a little kid who can't seem to be able to hold his head up and know there's going to be a better day tomorrow, it's really sad.*

Gary: *Do you try to intervene in those types of situations?*

Gabe: *I try to clear a way for them to be able to know there is still a choice to be made, but I can't always get through. So I am not able to console all of them.*

Gary: *Do you have help with this? Are there other people…*

Gabe. *Sure, there are so many souls here from your family, meaning yours and Mom's family that I have help from all the time. It's not my project alone.*

Gary: *What does the future look life for the earth, Gabe, as far as you're concerned?*

Gabe: *It's uncertain, because the future changes each second. It cannot be stuck in time long enough for us to know.*

Gary: *So, it would be difficult for anyone on earth to be able to predict this, let alone at your level to be able to predict this?*

Gabe: *Well, we think we know some times, but we can't be sure because the smallest change of action can produce an entirely* *different result and I don't know everyone's future. I can't believe you would want to.*

Gary: *I'm not sure I want to know everyone's future, I just want to know if there is a way that the people who are alive now in my generation can still make enough of a positive contribution to the world that we can impact positively the progressive changes that would be necessary to institute a turn around in those things that we don't want in our world?*

Gabe: *"Old people can be of help." I'm only kidding. All people can help or hinder the process.*

Gary: *Is there ever a way, Gabe, for you to know when someone special leaves the earth and transitions to your level, like this Mattie Stepanic?*

Gabe: *He's a cool guy. He's already joined us here and he's going to make —*

END OF TAPE

*Mom and Gabe at
Thomas Jefferson's
Monticello Home*

Gabe at Mammaw Callahan's Annual Christmas celebration with family

CHAPTER SIX

Confirming that We Weren't Losing our Minds

Dawn and I were advised by several people following the funeral services for our son that it would be wise to seek professional grief counseling. We knew this would be wise and yet we didn't know how it could possibly help because the true physical loss of our son had left such a deep, deep void within us. We didn't see how exchanging words, emotions, or stories could enable us to overcome that physical loss. Still, we followed the counseling path and chose to see a licensed professional pastoral counselor named Mark Williams, to whom we took an instant liking. Mark had a very open mind about life and life hereafter. We didn't know until we began to tell him about the messages that we were receiving that he had counseled many other people who had experienced similar situations, where they received communications from loved ones following their passing.

At first, I was concerned that Mr. Williams might have to report these private discussions to someone such as the health insurance company (which was picking up part of the tab for his services). I feared that we would be viewed as delusional. I knew my wife's employment could depend upon her stability, as her employer had just been acquired by a company known for taking extreme security measures with all of their employees.

When Mr. Williams indicated that he had counseled others with similar experiences, though not to the extent my wife and I had, he stated that most people simply don't know what to do with this type of information. They can't easily talk to their pastor or priest and they usually can't even seriously discuss the information with friends or family members who are likely to assume it is some mental delusion derived from intense emotional grief. So you're at risk talking about this with anyone. That's a fairly hopeless and helpless place to be following such a tragic loss.

Despite this, we have chosen to air openly with those that have an open mind our circumstances and explore the continued communications with Gabe, and with others. Our counselor felt that after five weeks, these communications had so positively impacted me that I had actually ascended spiritually to a higher place than where I was prior to Gabe's passing. Because of this, he saw no further reason for my involvement with him unless I elected to do so voluntarily, of course. He did say that time might effect my feelings differently, and that if I needed ever to return, I should do so at once.

My wife has not experienced the same benefit from these communications, due to the fact that she is the one providing the deepest medium channel for communications, through her experienced and gifted channeling abilities.

Despite the depth of the issues with our communications, she seldom can recall the messages and discussions as I do from the virgin inception of them through the intricacies of the discussions that we have with our son. Such depth of message that comes across from Gabe and others, which is shared through her so frequently, is often missed during the channeling by her. She can many times remember the emotions of the conversation from the other side, just not the telepathic exchange of information.

Yet, she is a very important reason that I am capable of healing so quickly (comparatively speaking). I owe her so much and will never be able to repay her in this lifetime for what she provides now to me through my son's most persuasive and instrumental, soulful and heartfelt, communications from the "other side."

While we continue to ponder where all this is taking us, and frankly, have wondered at times whether we were losing our minds to a degree by possibly just imagining that our dead son was communicating with us, two improbable and miraculous events (of so many now) occurred to provide objective proof that the messages from Gabe were real and verifiable:

Our son Noah had traveled with a group of his friends to a houseboat journey down at Dale Hollow, in Kentucky. Noah decided to go hang gliding over the water and while he was feeling the exhilaration, suspended in mid-air some thirty or thirty-five feet above water, he thought momentarily to himself, *"Gabe, I wish you could be here to enjoy and experience this with me. It is so much fun!"* At that very moment, Noah's glasses fell off and he was unable to catch them as they dropped into the water far below, where he lost them to the lake treasures forever. Even though he gave no further thought to Gabe after that time, Noah went back with the others to their boat to dry off and conclude the day by playing an electronic game called *Catch Phrase.*

The object of this game is to pass around an electronic device so that each player pushes a button that brings up one word. That one word then has to be used in such a way that people describe it without giving the word away, while the opponent attempts to guess what that word is.

Now the game has a database of some ten thousand words, Noah has told us. From the database, a word is randomly selected as you push the button. When the machine was handed to Noah and he pushed the button, much to everyone's amazement, the word *"Gabriel"* appeared!

Stunned, Noah's teammates looked at each other anxiously, wondering how Noah would respond, and what they should say or do. Noah just laughed and quipped, "I should have known that Gabe would be here with me at a time when I'm having so much fun!"

With the understanding that the game is entirely an electronic random selection without control of the database, the odds of the word "Gabriel" coming up would be ten thousand to one if we were strictly honoring the possibilities. But the probability — that of all people, Gabe's brother, Noah, out of the eight people who were playing this game — would be the person to draw that word out of a ten-thousand-word database on the first time around, is actually astounding by any scientific probabilities.

When Noah related this story to us upon his return, I could not help but notice that there was no fear, no questioning in his voice. Fear, I'm convinced, is what holds skeptics at such a distance from the opportunity of communicating with living spirits or souls.

If you have never seen God, how do you know that He exists? If you have never seen microwaves, how can you trust that they possibly work? If we cannot see radio waves or satellite communications frequencies, then…I think you see where this is going. We first must learn to open our minds, *to believe even when we cannot visually see conclusive evidence, that so much of our existence is unknown to so many of us.*

We need not believe that we must see to have understanding for our reality and/or our perceptions of what is real. *Our heart (love), our faith, and our compassion are all primary driving forces and essential ingredients to a wonderful, joyous, and happy life anywhere in the universe. This may be an oversimplification, and it may not! But what are the alternatives if we choose to ignore these forces as a way of life for us?*

In this world, fears that have been programmed into us by man's failure to comprehend or understand Gods entire universe and Plan, have, in fact, created confusion and uncertainty., Thoughts placed in our minds by cultural, or outdated thinking, religious mandates — some centuries old

— or science that seeks to prove hypotheses and theory by strictly hard data, are all ways that have taught us to demand that any existence must first have visual credibility before we can consider the possibility of making these thoughts possible for us to embrace in our value systems, and for us to think about our life in context of as a certain frame of reference for us.

To that I ask, show me the hard, cold proof that God exists. If we must work strictly from a visual standpoint, and not just the reasoning or justification for anything, then point God out to me now.

Perhaps, better yet, provide me with a personal autographed picture of him walking this earth. There is no absolute evidence that can prove man's beginning of existence for certain; or God's existence at all.

There is not enough certifiable, authentic information for scientists to conclude how or why we are here. So why do we accept preconditioned forms of thinking about such things that are unknown when all that these thoughts can truly do is provide poor frames of reference for us in our exploratory thinking?

By remaining open to these new matters of earthbound enlightenment, including the messages from this book, we will find our truths more quickly by examining the unknown, rather than by closing our minds to the possibilities.

Even a scientist should be intrigued, if not convinced, by what I am about to tell you. On the first day I returned to work following Gabe's funeral, as I drove up in our parking lot to our office on Monday morning at nine o'clock, I found several people outside scurrying around the landscaping outside of our office building, appearing to be searching for something. When I parked my car and got out, I was informed by my coworkers that the president of our company had been at the office late the night before, watering the fresh plantings around our new multimillion dollar facilities at our company, in Carmel, Indiana. Somehow in the late hours, around 10:00 PM, she had lost her diamond ring somewhere in the gardens surrounding the building.

A couple of feet of mulch extend out from our building with various plants, bushes, and trees arranged all the way around, making it very difficult to find any small object day or night. Jenny had searched for her diamond ring for three hours the night before with one other individual, with no success. Several other members of our company had come in early to begin the search that morning. Unfortunately, no one could locate the diamond ring. To make matters worse, we learned from Jenny that the ring was unscheduled and therefore uninsured for its approximate value of thirty-five thousand dollars. It was also a valued, sentimental gift.

After being unable to find the ring while joining in the search myself, I decided that this was serious enough that I would phone my wife to see if she could contact our son, though it had only been three days since we had buried him. It felt odd, but at the same time necessary, due to the sentimental value of the ring and its appraised monetary value. I felt that Gabe could help us.

I contacted my wife at home.

"Give me five minutes," she said, "and I will see if I can reach Gabe."

When she managed to reach Gabe and explained the circumstances, Gabe's response was "Mom!" and then there was a long pause.

"Gabe," my wife told him, "this is for your father and he needs your help. If you can do this, please do it for *him*."

There was no communication for a period of about thirty seconds, and then Gabe came back and gave Dawn a description of where the ring could be found, sitting partially buried in the mulch about one to two feet out from the base of the wall, which made it very difficult to locate.

Unfortunately, Dawn neglected to ask on which side of the building the ring could be found. So when I received the call from Dawn explaining where Gabe thought the ring was situated, I simply asked her to find out from Gabe whether it was in the front of the building, the side, or the back of the building.

She asked him and he responded: "Halfway between the door and the left side of the front of the building, near the base of the building."

Immediately, I hung up the phone, got up from my chair, and walked out the front door.

"Stop the search!" I yelled to Brian, one of my co-workers, who was still searching for the ring.

He looked at me very inquisitively as if to ask what on earth do you think you're doing?

"Don't move," I said in a firm voice. "I know where the ring is."

I didn't have an opportunity to look at Brian's face at that moment, but I imagine his expression would have been one of grave concern, even questioning how sane I was at that moment to call off the search, especially since I had been unable find it moments earlier.

Without hesitating, I took five complete steps toward the water faucet at the base of the building, reached down with my hand, and picked up the thirty-five-thousand-dollar diamond ring that no one else could find.

"How did you find that?" Brian exclaimed, amazed.

"Brian," I said, and then paused, I thought momentarily of giving him a fictitious story and then concluded that wouldn't be right, "my son told me where it was."

Brian stared vacantly at the ground and muttered, "Oh, okay."

I walked inside and handed the ring to our owner, who burst into tears. "How did you find it?" she asked me.

When I told her, she was so appreciative, that I sensed she recognized and accepted unquestioningly the miraculous means by which we discovered her ring. She felt badly that I had imposed on my son so shortly after he had died, yet elated that we had found this ring that meant so much to her.

The two events I have related above — Noah's experience with the word game and my finding the ring in the garden — convinced me that I was not crazy after all. A new force was at work in our lives. From that point on, I have no doubts about my sanity or my wife's sanity. In fact, it cannot be questioned, as far as I am concerned, as *imaginary* voices do not tell you where to find a ring that has been lost.

Since that time, we have located our missing dog by being given precise directions on where he was at ten-thirty at night (not missing one street or one turn of the wheel of the car); had our cat that ran away to die returned to us and laid in our locked garage, mysteriously. (I had prayed that we could see her one more time.)

We have learned about others who were sick or in trouble; and learned in advance where an affordable home was for my sister-in-law, Jill, and where she would ultimately relocate to. We have learned of where my nephew would attend college, eighteen months before he graduated from high school (committing to Texas A&M), even though he was only considering MIT, Cal-Berkely, Rice, Georgia, and Purdue at the time.

And so on, and so on, and so on. There are so many of these types of events that Gabe has helped us to better understand that the only thing left for Gabe to do that he hasn't yet done for us is to materialize for us to physically and visually see him once more.

Although he explained that he had not yet learned how to use his energy to do this, he could work with photon light energy and dust particles to create a picture on our downstairs hallway wall that would replicate his appearance while on earth. Because I had little understanding of how this could or would be done, I have had to investigate this to attempt to comprehend how my son was able to perform this master creation of himself (refer to the picture on the upper back cover of the book for the documentation of his creation).

In a somewhat difficult article to understand, I was able to learn more about this process through this excerpt of an article that I found that appeared on the internet, recently:

Photon light, sacred sound, noble gases
Important Aspects of Vibrational Energy Technology

By Linda Hannapel and Keith Frick

Opening the door to expanded awareness is best done by keeping things simple. After all, simplicity is the intrinsic nature of all universal principles. Vibrational Energy Medicine as eloquently discussed in Frank Geber's "Vibrational Energy Medicine," understands the simple fundamental nature of health and wellness as a vibrational relationship with the intelligence of the body. Everything is frequency vibration; frequency is the language of energy. All matter vibrates as energy; indeed, matter is nothing but energy. More specifically, matter is condensed light carried into physical manifestation by photons that are directed by creative intelligence.

Although Vibrational Energy Medicine is commonly thought of as acupuncture, homeopathy, aromatherapy, etc., it also includes therapeutic methods that apply frequency information directly to the body with color, sound, light, electricity, subtle, and magnetic energy.

This is the rapidly evolving field of Electromedicine, which includes a wide variety of Vibrational Energy Technologies.

We will discuss a remarkable type of frequency technology that involves the use of various "noble gases." These instruments nourish the body with a complete spectrum of bioavailable frequencies, while moving the lymphatic and circulatory systems to assist in detoxification. They also break up blockages and barrier tissues in the body by electrical repolarization. As the noble gases are ionized they emit "photon energy," reminding the body of the fundamental creative process.

Vibrational Energy Technologies can deliver frequency information more directly than the use of a substance or a remedy. This is because the energy lies closer to consciousness than matter; it is more universal and it has movement. Consequently, when the body receives energy and information directly, the results are far-reaching and broad in scope, without side effects.

One would best begin to describe the approach of Vibrational Energy Technology by understanding the language of energy, or frequency. All vibration is made up of energy pulsations of positive and negative polarity. We call that "frequency." It is the way we classify different expressions of energy.

The electromagnetic spectrum is a whole picture or a log of all the energy frequencies observed thus far. It is called "electromagnetic," because energy has both an electrical and magnetic component. The E/M spectrum then is a description of the energy frequencies from a few cycles per second to several million cycles per second. Low frequencies, for example, describe the electrical energy of brainwaves. A few hundred cycles per second is what we call sound: a few thousand per second are radio waves, and several million cycles per second are called light. So, from sound to light, there is a very broad range of frequencies. Color is simply a specific light frequency. Subtle energy and thought vibrations are known as Scalar Energy and could be considered a fourth-dimensional component of every third-dimensional vibration. Valerie Hunt? (couldn't read I) " The Science of Human Vibrations, " describes the aura as made up of low-frequency magnetic energy and intermediate and higher frequency electrical energy.

What are the most ideal frequencies to use? What kind of electrical energy best suits the body? Just as with any form of nutrition, wholeness is the key. Holistic approaches to health always provide a much broader range or possibilities. Therefore, presenting the body with a full band of frequencies is far more effective and comprehensive. Also, the quality of electrical current should match that of the body; the energy must be bioavailable.

The most recent evolution in Vibrational Energy Technology advances the research of Tesla, Rife, Abrams, and Lakhovsky by combining several instruments in one. Although there are many different types of frequency instruments to address a large variety of mental and physical health issues, noble gas technology offers profound advantages. As mentioned, when these special gases contained in glass tubes are ionized, a powerful photon-rich electrical field is sent out into the air. A micro-current containing millions of harmonic frequencies gently penetrates the body through the skin. In addition a radio-wave component may be added to carry the frequencies and subtle energy through the body without any distortion. In this way, a comprehensive delivery of energy is achieved containing a holistic spectrum of photobiotic nutrition.

Because the micro-current emitted from the noble tubes matches the electrical properties of the body, it is able to travel along both the subtle and gross energy channels. This includes the energy pathways of the consciousness and those on the molecular level, as well as the acupuncture meridians, the lymph channels and blood vessels. Thus the gentle, yet penetrating photon energy fills the entire body as life-force energy rich in frequency harmonics.

The same electrical energy also breaks up bound protein matter and cells which have lost their normal electrical charge. When the cells of our bodies lose their normal charge, they gather together and form clumps and clots rather than maintain their individual integrity. Rare gas technology can rapidly restore the normal energy state and ideal frequency to every cell in the body.

Every cell also resonates a unique characteristic frequency. This is why it is important to ionize the noble gases with frequencies that are rich in harmonics. In other words, universal frequencies of Sacred Sounds are most ideal. These are frequencies which lie in the mid-sound range, and decades of research have shown that they carry the most abundant simultaneous harmonic frequencies. In this way, each cell is able to match its own resonate frequency amidst a vast array of harmonic frequencies. Finally, noble-gas tube technology delivers a powerful electrical field that restores the circulation of all the fluids in the body, especially the lymph and blood. The lymphatic system is connected to every organ in the body and is absolutely essential in purifying the body and strengthening the entire immune system. Many consider the proper lymphatic drainage to be even more important than blood circulation. These fluids, however, require the pumping actions of movement and exercise, which is often severely limited in modern lifestyles.

Perhaps, the most profound value of noble-gas technology lies in the exotic healing value of the gases themselves. Not only do these special elements provide an excellent medium for the transfer of an electrical field of energy, they also provide an access to what is called ether, or the "gap," as Deepak Chopra calls it. Allowing the full-frequency electrical energy to travel across air and ether inside glass tubes adds a unique multidimensional component. It is within this gap that photon energy can be expressed in its primordial state, acting just as it does in the expansive void of intergalactic space. It is here that the essence of these most stable elements comes alive.

Noble gases (helium, argon, neon, xenon, krypton) are the most unique of all the elements in the universe. They are called the inert of rare gases because they are completely balanced in their number of electrons, protons, and neutrons. They do not easily react or combine with other elements. These special gases were once far more abundant in the atmosphere. Many believe these gases act as windows to other dimensional realities and are integral to higher states of consciousness that once prevailed on earth. Walter Russel, renowned spiritual scientist, described the noble gases as holographic representatives of all the other elements in the universe, or "octaves of integrating light." Ascended Master Hilarion, as channeled by John Fox and others, attributes specific healing and spiritual properties to each noble gas. Xenon, for example, opens us up to higher states of consciousness and regenerates the body. Whereas, argon clears away negative thought-forms and has been the most thoroughly researched in the treatment and alleviation of infections. Krypton is noted to improve psychic abilities and improve brain function. Helium connects one to dream states and can alleviate insomnia. Most of these properties have been substantiated by personal experience and clinical research.

Photon energy is the other key element of the regenerative and rejuvenating value of noble gas technology. Photobitotic nutrition is the nutrition of light. It is the photon light energy we receive directly from the sun, or secondarily, from our food. *Photons emerge from the nonphysical realms and are the messengers of creative intelligence.* All electromagnetic phenomena moves, manifests and changes through the exchange of photons on a quantum level.

When the body is exposed to this primordial expression of photon energy as the gases are ionized, it is reminded of the essential creative process of consciousness enlivening energy which then precipitates as matter.

Once my good friend and attorney, Bill Green, learned of the extraordinary messages being received by Gabe, he phoned two leading scientists involved in the study of afterlife consciousness and paranormal activity, who spoke with him about different means of scientifically testing Gabe to see if this was a reality or an illusion. Bill asked me to secure Gabe's permission to address this type of test with him.

Gabe replied, " Dad, we are not hear to conduct magic acts like a magician would perform, and we don't feel the need to seek approval by scientifically enabling the evidence of our existence to be brought to earth. Quite the contrary, actually, as we want people to deepen their faith first to open their hearts and minds to our existence, without appearing in the physical, or moving objects, etc. Besides, we mostly conduct our affairs by soulful thought energy and telepathy."

With that knowledge, Bill arranged a test for Gabe, which Gabe consented to participate in, at my most adamant plea-bargaining moments with him, actually, to set the record straight for Bill, once and for all.

Gabe knew that I believed and understood the communications were real, but he felt that Bill and Dan did not, and therefore, because it was important to me that they believed, he would consent to Bill's test.

He told me that, no matter what the results were, that Bill would not believe them. When I asked why, he stated, "Bill demands visual proof, Dad, and cannot bring himself to have this type of faith in his reality, yet. Perhaps, one day he will, though."

Still, at a precise time on a Friday evening, I called on Gabe, and he appeared to respond to Bill's idea for the test. I said, "Bill wants you to visit Dan Stenger's home in McClean, Virginia, and look in on what Dan has written in the way of a number for you to communicate back to us." We had a conference call, and all of us were enthusiastically awaiting the results.

Gabe said that this would take about sixty seconds, and he should be back to communicate with us. (I'd love to travel that quickly from near-Indianapolis to near-Washington D.C. Can you imagine the amount of time we would save?

He returned in one minute and recited the set of numbers that Dan had written down on a tiny piece of paper. Sadly for me, Gabe missed four of the five numbers, and actually did poorer than you or I could have done with this same test, in all probability.

Everyone seemed disappointed, and I was confused by the results; until I asked Gabe, "What happened, why did you miss so many numbers?" He replied, "Dan wrote them in such small print that I couldn't make out most of them. However, I did notice that, laying on the kitchen table where he was sitting, were a number of objects that were lying on the table."

To my astonishment, I asked, "What were they?" He named eight of the objects and one of the objects' specific color. They included a bible, a pair of glasses, a book, a towel, a newspaper, and some trinkets that Dan instantly denied were sitting on the table; that is, until he lifted the newspaper up and found them sitting underneath it!

We were all astonished at the accuracy of Gabe's ability to name these objects, let alone to cite where Dan was sitting, when he wrote the numbers out for Gabe to attempt to read.

Dan became a believer that night, and Bill still wanted more evidence! Gabe was right, Bill wasn't ready to accept this on faith! And his right to refuse to accept this was keeping him from ever truly knowing the depth of these remarkable events or their true importance for all of us.

Skepticism will diminish most everything, if tolerated. I love Bill, but, to this day, I feel that he has some reservations based on a lack of true visual or cognitive evidence that he still requires, rather than requiring faith to be his guiding light in the absence of certainty of knowledge.

So, while we soon understood that we were not hallucinating or delusional at all, our grief counselor verified this for us, and we learned this on our own, also.

Our contact with Gabe was, and is still, certain. No other tests are, or were necessary for us. Because of this, we politely turned down several offers to travel to test sites in Arizona, North Carolina, and Georgia, through university-funded programs, mostly to test the afterlife-consciousness theory that has yet to be supported by scientific evidence that has been universally accepted. We knew that Gabe didn't feel it was necessary for this testing, as it would never satisfy the "critics," and we no longer felt it was important, either.

In trying to find the most significant way to express to others what all of this has been about so far, in just a few short words, I looked to Gabe again, one day, for the answer. I said, "Gabe, how would it be best for me to conclude this chapter in summary if this is all that the book and I have to offer to this point?"

And here is what he told me to relate to you: "Life is not about that which we know...it is about that which we have yet to discover."

Gabe visiting the ancestral burial grounds for the Vaught family located near Somerset KY – (over 150 years old)

Gabe and good friend Robbie at our family home

CHAPTER SEVEN

Sorting Out the Lessons That We Are to Learn from this Entire Experience.

I've always thought of my life as a journey and one that has never been fulfilled or completed to the greatest extent because I always find so many things I have yet to do; things that I've wanted to accomplish in my life, but haven't yet.

Gabe has made it a point to say to us through our communications that the messages that we receive from him will serve to enlighten us in an advanced way, if we will only give them careful consideration.

As he stated just recently, "You asked for success in this lifetime, Dad. You have also wanted to be on the leading edge of all futuristic knowledge as a messenger and interpreter of the information for others. You have been granted theses wishes.

"By Divine intervention, and direct work with The Holy Spirit, you will be given information to interpret and pass on for your personal development, and the development of others in the world." He went on to say, "Isn't this what you want, Dad?"

Gabe reminded me of my responsibilities to all who care to listen and to know of these Holy messages.

"Dad, here's how it works: you are given the information by me or directly by a Higher Spirit, perhaps Jesus. Then, you give the information to others as you can best relate it to them. This requires you to understand the clarity of the messages, and then their importance to you and others, and then to interpret them as well as you can for others to learn and benefit from."

It really is a significant responsibility for me, and a difficult challenge to realize all that I must learn myself before trying to provide any source of uncommon knowledge to others. It has been exhausting, at times, and yet, so sweet and wonderful for me.

I asked Gabe, "Why do people feel the need to question me, Gabe, when I am simply doing my best to enlighten them about these profound messages that I receive?"

He said, "Dad, unless Christ himself revealed himself to all, in the physical sense, anything that anyone would say on His behalf would not only be questioned, but rejected by many." This made sense, as I grew up learning that so many had rejected Him when He was still here in human form!

"Why," I asked, "does this have to happen,, Gabe?"

He responded by saying, "Human beings fear what they don't know, or, what might create major changes in their life for them. So often, major changes are needed in their life, and you will help plant the seeds for many to move forward and progress with this information, even though it will not come easy for you."

He had once before told me, "Dad, you are a lot like Johnny Appleseed, in that you will plant seeds wherever you go with your teaching, your casual conversations, and your requirements to help others as you are directed to do. But you will never see the fruits of your labor in this lifetime, Dad.

The best that you can hope for is that you will one day recognize your achievements from the work that you are doing now and know that it was meaningful to some, and brought about a new awareness for others.

"Your challenges will be many. Your personal gratification will come only from your knowledge that you are doing what many will not do, or, will not understand how to do. In any event, you have chosen this for your life's work. Carry on and let tomorrow take care of tomorrow. Just do the best that you can in the moment and know that I am so proud of your efforts, Pop!"

Another major lesson that I learned through conversations with my son is the difference between good and evil. By definition, as it relates to how human beings perceive these two contrasting elements; "good," we typically refer to as the essence of what we desire and strive to be, or be like, as in "good people." In a very general sense, we all want to be "good" at something.

At the same time, humans generally feel that "evil" is considered to be anything that we generally "dislike or feel unsafe with, or tempted by, or frightened by."

Gabe has made it a point to educate me with the understanding that "good" and "evil" must exist in our world, because they serve to "balance one another at all times." God's greatness is also found in the balance of all things. However, "evil doesn't really exist. It is simply the absence of goodness."

Example: If the world had too much "good," and not enough perceived "evil," as he explained to me in one conversation, "there would be an imbalance, because human beings would perceive even good things at the very lowest levels to be closer to 'evil,' the contrasting thought process in our spectrum of thinking. And just as yes has no, day has night, happiness has sadness, and love has fear, so must there be a balance of good and the absence of good on earth for all of our continued educational needs." We learn from everything, not just from one end of the spectrum of thought or life.

In essence, "evil" (the absence of good) is no accident, either. We tend to label "evil" in a manner that makes it seem like it's the work of an awful or terrible force, and at times, the tragedy (or the perception of) "evil" seems that way under the most tragic of circumstances.

But God permits there to be balance in all things. Although Gabe told me that "Satan does not exist," he also stated that "darkness – the absence of God's light," does exist. However, it is so, because certain spirits do not choose to raise their levels of awareness and ascend toward God or the Light. They covet the lowest vibrations of all of life and remain there, without any knowledge or devotion toward heading toward the Light, or the highest energy that they can comprehend moving toward. It is an act of ignorance and faithlessness, and for those who cannot or will not change, similar to a living hell.

"Hell is a manmade perception," Gabe acknowledged early in our conversations. On earth, we tend to want to formulate easy-to-recall images in our mind when we associate something or another with good (or the absence of good). So we conjure up ideas that we allow our earliest programming to provide to us, and we spend our lifetime living with these early perceptions without really reexamining their truth or value to us now to any degree.

All spirits — yours, mine, and all who live in the afterlife — have defined energy levels based on Light energy (God's energy), and we function based on the principles that we have embraced and chosen to accept, or not. So when we have major issues that occur in the world (on the physical plane of earth), they are a direct result of how people are thinking, acting, and caring (or not caring), from moment to moment, collectively.

What we have then is an accumulation of our total life individual energy's built through our lifetime of practices that we embrace, and the collective energy on earth of every other spirit, and those beliefs which they are, or are not, embracing. For those who want to understand the solutions to the complexity of this life formula to a simpler degree, know that divine intervention, angelic assistance, and spiritual communications can also serve as enlightenment to those who allow their ears and their hearts to truly acknowledge the existence of these afterlife energy forces.

The lower the practice of light energy — love, kindness, consideration for others, suspension of judgment, faith in God, faith in our fellow man, trust, and hope, etc. — then the less our chances of solving any or many of the world's most difficult challenges today. It is an easy formula to understand, and a hugely difficult formula to change. Why?

Mankind resists change whenever possible. He prefers a comfort zone, a path of the least resistance. This means that we prefer no earth-shaking information, no matter how truthful it is; nothing that will require "me" to use additional energies to convert my misperceptions of life, or thinking processes that I have grown accustomed to exercising, into something more significantly healthy or useful to us. We prefer to remain afloat more often than we submerge our thoughts into deeper, clearer, waters.

Just as all information comes to me when I most need it, just the other day, I opened a file on the Internet, and here is what I read: "First, they will ignore you. Then, they will laugh at you. Then, they will fight with you. And then, you win." (Gandhi).

Since Gabe's death, I have begun to examine more closely what is really meaningful to me and what the most important aspects of what I want to spend the next several years of my life focusing on and giving my energies to, are.

Among the many messages that I have been given from Gabe since his passing, the most meaningful messages have been those that have talked about the following things:

(1) Living each second as fully as possible in the spirit of Jesus Christ

(2) Giving and receiving to the greatest possible extent unconditional love at all times to all people

(3) Remembering that kindness will overcome so many problems and difficulties in our lives and that I need to exercise compassion and acceptance for others and compassion and acceptance for myself, consistently.

And the most recent message which has had a great impact, and I still consider quite often, is the message that came on Father's Day (2004), when I asked my son if he would like to give me additional information that I might want to put into the content of the book to pass along to future readers. His remarks were "Glory be to God," and he went on to indicate "God is everything and everything is God." From the smallest little detail that we can and cannot understand to the greatest details that we can and can't understand, God has created and is all of these things through his energy, which is: love.

Human beings live each day mostly without thinking about God as a part of their spirit and their spirit as a part of God. My son indicated that God was a spark within each of us (the Kingdom) that can allow us to perform and accomplish many things in our lives with the complete acceptance of God in all things. He further stated *that is not necessary to honor God, but to know him, because God is God and God is good.* By knowing God we do honor the energy and spirit of God.

However, it is important to remember at all times the glory of God in all things. For all things are precious and all things are here by his creation, not by accident. There are no accidents. Not one accident has ever occurred on earth to my son's knowledge. All events, people, animals, plants, and life forms are His. All nanoseconds have a purpose for each and every one of us. It is our destiny to learn what these experiences represent and what they mean to our growth and development and life eternal. "This is why we come to the earth to live," Gabe has chided. "We can experience what we have not learned yet, here, and take those experiences and meld them with our previous knowledge and wisdom."

The details of these messages, at the time they were given to me, were so unexpected and so deep, and intimately personal, that today I still wonder about them and think about them a great deal for the educational wisdom that they hold.

What was my son trying to tell me and what did he want me to know to the greatest possible extent with these messages, early on?

I believe now that it was simply to *have faith that all things are as they should be.* That doesn't mean that life won't get better, it just means that, in order for all of us to learn what we need to know, we must accept our current positions in life until we are ready to change and progress onward in our personal development.

Each of us make that decision for ourselves, based on when it feels right to do so! Time will determine who moved on and who didn't, and whether it had any relevance to anything else at all in the universe.

While there were certainly direct and personal messages for Dawn and me, so many of the messages contained what I perceived to be a duality of messages for others who care to know more about the afterlife.

For this reason, I began to realize that these messages are not always my own personal messages. Rather, they are my own personal messages to share so often as others can grow with them and experience their divine and physical realities for each of us to use as we best can to improve our quality of life.

In a sense, the messages belong to everyone who can, and who chooses to, believe in something greater than their own existence and base of knowledge, presently.

They are for those who are willing to receive new and uncommon information openly into their heart and mind to explore their own creation and purpose here.

In our very earliest communications, when Gabe mentioned "living in the Spirit of Christ," I was so profoundly moved by the importance of that knowledge that my recollection of that moment was that I became so intensely introspective at that very thought, wondering, why now and why me?

It was as if my higher consciousness was being awakened to recall what I had repressed for some unknown reason thus far in my life here. And, now, allowing me to use the information for my own good and for the good of others, to grow beyond where I had come to in my life and the direction for my life at that moment. *I was being blessed because of my faith in something greater than myself, my faith in God.*

I began to examine what I thought were potential deficiencies and/or mistakes that I had made, where I had not utilized that thought process as my guiding force in my life. And then my son, in his exceptional wisdom, reminded me again, "Dad, there are no such things as mistakes on earth. People want to believe this to protect their ego when rejection, pain, or consequences revolve around various events in their lives. But, everything was charted and decided as to what outcomes might occur despite the many ways of determining the nature of the outcomes *through the God-given blessing of free will for everyone.*"

Bumper stickers that I read sometimes while traveling on the interstate, that line the backs of many cars say "What would Jesus do?" This has helped me to realize how meaningful now that thought-process really is to my life.

It helps me to assume different perspectives that remind me of the Light, and my son's previous comments. It is one thing to know the figurative meaning of something we value and to analyze it and dissect it when convenient, and it is an entirely different matter when we can understand, to a higher degree through our experiences, what the literal interpretation of that something really means to our life.

It is my belief that, for those people who truly live in the Sprit of Christ, it is not a "sometimes" thing.

It is a practice that requires great meditation, great listening skills, great observation skills, and the ability to practice great love for all mankind and all creation. It means giving up all distractions and associations and one's premise (self-illusion) of their personal identity through their ego-based perceptions of themselves, most often.

*Visiting Great, Great ,Uncle Roosevelt (95 yrs young) and Great, Great,
Aunt Pearly, and their son and his wife, Mr.and Mrs. Vernon Vaught, and
Gabe's Great Uncle Bob and Great Aunt Pat, and Grandma and Grandpa
Vaught, and Dad, at Uncle Roosevelt's farm near Somerset, KY*

Gabe's Eighth-grade school class photo

CHAPTER EIGHT

How, and Why, We Should Incorporate The Possibilities Here Into Our Life

Executing giving up one's normal thought processes through the meditative application of visualization of the absence of anything and everything allows for one's higher consciousness and awareness to break through and guide the mind through one's heart and soulful purpose, through one's higher consciousness, again.

Applying these precious practices, to the extent that it means giving up one's ego and one's personal desires at times for the good of the examination of what our higher calling really is, is a key to learning how to live in the Spirit of Christ.

His Spirit does not create our distractions. Our ego-dominated thinking processes (combined with our emotional tendencies) are often undisciplined forms of limitations that we all have to learn to work with while on earth, and are what creates our *lostness*, more often and confusion.

We are challenged to overcome distractions that can lead us away from His Spirit, through perceptions of self-defeat, victimization, perpetual sadness or depression, and/or insecurities that block our ability to grasp how great and powerful we really are as living spirits and human beings.

To learn how to assume control of our spiritual evolution and development, we must first learn to give up any efforts to control our pathways or others' pathways in life.. Our natural development will then take its place in our life.

The only solid reason that I can think of that would create a desire for any of us to want to control anything in this world is that we feel inferior, inadequate, or helpless to otherwise manage our life by managing only ourselves. In an ego-based world, that is a liability. In a God centered world, that is the farthest end of the spectrum from what God has created for us, and what truly exists for us to be happy and at peace within ourselves.

He (God) is our Light and we are the Light that exists as a result of living in our reflection of our faith in Him, (the energy of God). We move toward the Light or away from the Light with each and every nanosecond of our life on earth.

By our thinking and our intentions and our subsequent actions that manifest our intentions, we determine our fates at any given second. The accumulation of our intentions are what bring us prosperity or danger as we think of these things in our physical existence here on earth..

We grow the fastest from learning to choose to live our life through The Universal Spirit. Though seldom will we give up our need for our personal identity (illusionary), as we all want to feel that we are greater in spirit than another by prompting our ego to create that illusion. The need for the feeling of superiority becomes a liability to our spiritual growth, as we dismiss the feelings that we are all one and special as just that.

I was told that our ego's are illusions that we create for our own purposes. They distinguish us from others(in an unbalanced way), and therefore, create the illusion that we are all separate creatures from one another and God. That's how conflict and battle and wars are started, and continue to this day. If we felt that we were all one with the universe, who would seek to discredit or destroy one another, or the world, itself?

While I think of myself as a person who spends more time living in the Spirit of Christ these days, the fact of the matter is, I haven't always spent my time there, and I certainly haven't always practiced what I have learned here, either.

But since the time my son has spoken to me about this, I have focused as much as I will with the awareness that I have on what living this way means to my life — the rewards and the positive outcomes that result from living in His Spirit.

The wonderful feelings every day that result from the "goodness" that I experience when I step into the flow of relinquishing control of my life egocentricities and the material desires that seem to dominate earth now, help me to grow in a God centered focus and reality more and more.

I am not alone, however, and many others are joining the desire for balance in all things in our life.. I couldn't imagine thinking of all of this, or presenting all of this, without Divine Intervention and His Holy guidance, daily. All spiritual guidance is a grant of humanity for humanity, if used to experience life in a meaningful and blessed way each day.

When I am not listening to or being consumed by my ego, I find that the river of good fortune does indeed flow through my door of life and on to others for their good fortune, as well.

I don't have to carry those heavy burdens of uncertainty or the balls and chains that I use to constrain the possibilities of becoming a better human being and contributor to the goodness of this world. When I allow my ego to dominate my life and others, I commit to living with the prospect that this is the best that I will ever be.

I cannot recognize the true limitations that I place on myself or others from that frame of reference. As a result, I diminish the hope that I have of growing beyond the limitations that I have, and I reduce the possibilities of allowing others to learn through my leadership, my association with them, and my example to them.

There are blessings that will come to me by learning to ask for help and to believe (have faith) that it will come, though perhaps not on my schedule or by my anticipated plans.

This often reminds me of the cute anecdote, "God grant me patience...and give it to me now!" So often, we demand confirmations of our blessings immediately, and so, seek to find them in our own time, rather than through the natural order of life. That is our ego's way of acquiring self-gratification.

As a result of Gabe's information and guidance to me, I no longer pray to God or Christ for material blessings. I now pray that I may reach out to grasp the Spirit of God by living a natural life in the practice of His world, His thoughts, and His goodness and not just relishing these thoughts and words, themselves.

I was informed by another spiritual source in the afterlife that we all have spirit guides and angel guides that we can turn to for prayer, not just God or Christ or Buddha, etc., when we seek their intervention and assistance in our life.

I was told that each of us has a different number of spiritual guides, but most of us have seventy-five or so guides to rely on to help us during our earth experience.

Some of them help us with finances, matters of the heart, compassion, problem-solving, avoiding accidents that can alter our destiny, growing in our spiritual awareness, etc. We think the world is full of coincidences daily, when in fact, there are no coincidences. We have a universe full of assistance and intervention, each and every second that we live, to guide us to and through our lessons that we are here to learn. They cannot interfere with our free will, however, unless they are asked to do so by us or the divine power. Living in the Light continuously allows them full authority and access to help us, however, for this is the divine way of living.

It has been reinforced to me that words are only symbols to God. Symbols are only meaningful if and when they are lived and practiced as a way of life (through our intentions).

We can pretend that our words are useful to us; however, they are useless unless they are reinforced by our actions. In any matter, words are still less useful, because when we use our actions, our actions speak so much more loudly than our words.

It is through my son's messages that I have begun to realize the simplicity of life: say what you mean to say, and do what you say you will do, so that your actions and your words are congruent. Make feelings of love and compassion the center of all of your actions, and prosper as never before. By doing these things, you to take full responsibility for your life, your ways of living, your intentions, and reduce uncertainty and ambiguousness to create inner peace in your soul.

This allows everyone to better know the real you (just as you are), to love you, and to accept you for who you truly are. They don't have to live with the fear of misreading your feelings, not knowing your intentions, or misunderstanding or misinterpreting your love and acceptance for them.

There are no disguises or need for disguises when you're comfortable living in the Holy Spirit. You communicate in what we commonly associate as a supernatural way, to some degree, through His presence of love.

The rewards of conferring with the afterlife, in particular, my son, have reduced my stress many times over. I have learned to trust myself first. Then, I have met neighbors whom I never really knew. I have met strangers I would have never known, just by going out of my way to say something pleasant to them. They have become more than strangers and so; many have become friends, instinctually, to me.

I have a deeper appreciation for and love for all mankind that did not exist previously. I am becoming more of what I wanted for myself, just by being myself and being grateful for who "I am." I no longer have a desire or need for pretense or arrogance. They are superficial and major limitations in our life to our development toward becoming an advanced (Light) soul.

I personally pray each day, several times a day, and need to make more time for this if I intend to grow in God's Spirit even more.

I have attended as many as three classes a week on gaining further spiritual enlightenment through meditation. These classes include working with experienced clairvoyants, trans-mediums, and God-centered, thinking people. I've enjoyed them all; like attracts like on this earth.

Recently, I have had to reexamine many close, personal relationships that I developed throughout my life. All have been so meaningful to me throughout my life, and, because of changes that I have become aware of now, some friendships will require my letting go of these relationships, from past experiences that have meant so much to me, to develop new friendships to work with and to learn from and to guide me in newfound life experiences.

I learned that all relationships are important and play a critical role in our life. Those relationships that don't work out teach us so much, just as the others do. At different times in our life, we must learn something from every relationship, good or bad. We will even learn important information from chance encounters with others that we may have only once in our lifetime.

In doing this, I'll likely have to pass on the time investment with many of the same people I've always valued as my closest associates and friends. There is a time for coming and a time for going through all of life's relationships. This includes the time invested with family, sometimes.

In the world, there are at least two contrasting models for living. I was speaking with my brother-in-law recently, who is a doctor of psychology, and he was describing for me the different life syndromes that people choose when they are seeking a means by which to live as a way of life for themselves.

For so many there is the "survival" model. Never changing, never caring enough to change, and wanting only to keep one's head above the waterline for fear of drowning are common symptoms of this way of thinking.

For those who live in this way of thinking, survival is a precarious and uncertain day-to-day chore. I was thinking, however, that the "survival" model isn't just for financially poor people, as it relates to customs and habits and spiritual development here on earth; not just someone's personal inadequacies or financial problems.

The second model, at the other end of the spectrum, is the "thrive" model. I thought, when people learn to live in the Spirit of God as a way of life, they always seem to thrive on life. Do they have problems? Absolutely! Do they face the same types of daily obstacles as others? Absolutely! Then how do they thrive?

They seem to place their uncertainties, their worries, their lack of faith, their hopelessness, and their thoughts of victimization, into God's laundry basket each morning. And at the end of the day, they find that their dirty laundry has been washed and cleaned, and their hearts are free from the problems and the instability of carrying those issues around with them every moment of every day.

They ask God to walk with them and hold away from them those mental creations which we, as human beings, are famous for using to sabotage our own happiness and success with our life. They " thrive" on goodness aspects of their life, and they choose to center their attention on contributions to others daily, not strictly on their problems or concerns!

They leave behind the "survival" thinking processes that are so hard to outgrow or overcome, once you become addicted to that way of thinking. You can have millions of dollars and still choose to live in the "survival" model as a way of life. I have relatives that still do this. They never seem to have enough! Sadly, they never will, unless they change the way that they are thinking about living and prospering through God, not their bank accounts.

I recently was reminded that every single love story in our lifetime ends in tragedy for someone. I hadn't given that any real thought until the afterlife source brought it to my attention; to better help me cope with my son's death, I suppose.

The daily grind of all of our life experiences, our own personal time tables, and small and large perceived crises all form a part of what our bigger-picture reasons are for being here on earth. Without daily prayer, we are attempting to manage our life alone. At some point, it becomes futile and unlikely that we will succeed this way.

We don't have enough information available to us to foresee the events that we are here to learn from. We need guidance to help us in finding those events, then working through those events all throughout our life here.

I could not find time for introspection and reflection without taking time for myself in prayer. By some degree, I would be lessening the significance of my reason for being here by not living up to my pursuit of my truest potential (my higher purpose). Gabe helped me to realize that all that is real lies in prayer and in growing closer to the Light, the divine, God.

My son has also reminded me, during many of these communications, that the best basis for measuring where one is with one's spiritual development is not to measure where you were yesterday, or where you are today, but the direction in which you are heading now, overall, with your intentions, your purpose for living, and your actions each moment that you are here. Some improvement, any improvement, is better than no improvement at all. We all must start somewhere in making those changes to improve by including the guiding forces in our daily life. Not to do this is analogous to one's fear of quitting smoking. It may seem difficult at first, but it is the lifeline that keeps you growing rather than dying.

I have learned that we cannot fulfill our true destiny without seeking a higher spiritual God and purpose for our life. Whether we are believers as Buddhists, Hindus, Jews, Christians, or other faiths and religions, we only reach our highest being on earth through stretching to reach the

Highest Being that we honor in our spirit, in our faith, and in our quest for universal energy development.

In this way, all faiths are really the same. They speak to the same considerations, only in different perspectives, through different levels of awareness, in different languages, while attempting to differentiate themselves from others, unfortunately.

Differences are the diversity that God created for us to learn from, not reject! Just as he created lions, tigers, bears, dogs, and so many other beautiful forms of life, he wanted acknowledgement and respect for all of His creation. It is because it is, and because He created it like this.

Why must we question the differences, rather than embrace the commonality of our existence here, and hereafter? Rather than asking, why? We should ask, "why not"? (Kennedy's own reminder to us nearly four decades ago)

I love so many of the words that Einstein spoke, because they have such timeless truth to them. There is a well-known passage from his reflections on mankind that stated "with the advent of the atom bomb, all things have changed, except how men think."

This is exactly why implementing changes on earth are so difficult to do socially. It is why the ever-present and ominous possibilities exist for a nuclear war. Bertrand Russell and Albert Einstein warned "there can be no winners in a nuclear war." But do we listen? Are we listening with our hearts? Einstein also stated, "I know how World War II was fought, I know not how World War III will be fought, but, I know how World War IV will be fought — with sticks and stones."

It only takes one nuclear bomb to make for a sad day for any and all of us. I believe his words are prophetic. He was considered to be a genius. With these concerns for mankind, it is easy to understand why so many respect his thinking.

To people who are fundamentalists (in a religious sense), much of this book will be a striking and controversial subject matter that no doubt will meet with great opposition. I have only to gain the self-satisfaction of knowing and sharing this truth through the publication of this critical information, in some cases.

As one person, you or I can change another's way of thinking. If not, we are all headed for a one-way ticket out without the hope of leaving a better world to our future generations. Our world not only depends on people speaking out like this on matters of life existence, but our collective spiritual development literally depends on our listening to all of the possibilities, here and hereafter.

Change isn't just an idealistic means for viewing our world. This is the evidential hope that gives the world many second opportunities to correct itself, correct the imbalances, foster goodwill toward others, and remake our society into something more beautiful, universally.

In instituting change, we can instantly reverse the Light imbalance by bringing a higher level of vibration and energy to our world with a higher level of thinking (through the Spirit of God), and bring about a new day all at once, for everyone on earth.

This is similar to what occurs when parts of the world pray together in vigilance for one cause or another. The collective energy unites and sends the energy vibration of the world to a higher level creating more Light and understanding and raising the ability for man and God to manifest these changes that will guide the earth's destiny to a better place for all, for all of time.

Our thoughts are what put into action our initiatives and creates all end results for ourselves and our world in every task or matter that we undertake. If we fail to make changes in our thinking, changes for hope, for our future quests as a civilization, we confine ourselves to having what we have always had. War, tyranny, greed, instability between nations, hopelessness for so many; all of this comes about simply because we refuse to change! We choose then "not to care enough to institute change."

Two fundamental factors can change our world instantly. Both are essential, however, only one is really necessary at all times. "Caring is the existence of God's very Essence." When we fail to care, we leave our lives open to less than what we many times want for ourselves or others. Only "knowledge and caring" will save the world for others to enjoy. However, given these facts, "only caring will result in the perpetual chance for life, when we are without the knowledge that we need most."

This is true because, "when we care to learn what it is that we do not understand or know, we will learn what it is that we do not understand or know." In the meantime, we must exercise our passion for caring for and accepting our world as it is, for what it truly is, and not that which we simply hope for it to become.

I believe my son with all my heart. I believe in everything he's telling me that I am capable of understanding clearly and consciously. No one on the other side, who lives in the Light of God, is permitted to deceive others and still progress toward the Light (God). I have recently learned of my son's progressive transitional spiritual development by four additional levels since his transition to the "other side." Keep in mind that, for every level one advances to in life (here or hereafter), there are approximately one million lessons that must be learned (in human terms). Ever wonder how much progress we are collectively making?

My son assured me that there is no literal "hell," but just a mindset that we can achieve through lower processes of thinking and lower level vibrational practices that we continue to carry out at any given moment in our life, here, or hereafter.

In that same conversation with my son, he indicated that after you have reached the other side in transition and you have been there a period of time for adjustments, you select a time for a "complete review of your entire life," with yourself and God as your witness.

Because the other side vibrates so much faster (five times faster) than we do here on earth, you are able to review every aspect, every moment, everything you've ever said or done in your life all during a specific period of time that allows you to look, feel, and experience once again all those moments that you lived on earth. So whatever you embraced as your way of life, at any given time in life, becomes your life lessons to learn from your experiences on earth.

If you chose to be kind and loving, or mean and dispirited, or a combination of these things at various intervals of your life, there are insights that you draw from that and lessons that you are to learn that illuminate your soul (Light body) and provide for you the next lesson(s) that you need to learn, hereafter.

It is at that time that you determine what you have gained in knowledge and in enlightenment from the lessons that you learned while experiencing the "teaching zone" that we call earth.

Did you meet the needs of your higher purpose when coming back to earth? Did you learn from these experiences and grow closer to God? Or, did you move away from God, refusing to live in His ways, and choosing your ego as the epicenter of all of your life actions and experiences? After all, you were provided your free will to determine what choices you wanted to make with your life.

You decide for yourself the path that is yours. You may take the path of least resistance, or, the path with the greatest challenges. In the Spirit world, those who experience the greatest challenges in life, and learn from them the lessons for their life, are those who advance their souls most rapidly into new life learning opportunities, all the while growing closer to the Light.

So, the next time you see the homeless on the streets, or the quadriplegics in the wheelchairs or in the hospitals, or the mentally disabled in day-to-day life experiences, remember who the fortunate ones really are. Think of it in terms of sacrifice., and what rewards lie in the hereafter for them.

From those experiences on earth, you reveal to yourself the amount of growth and development that occurred, if any, during your time on earth as a human being. I asked my son if all human beings advance and develop when they return from earth and he stated "no," that did not necessarily always occur.

He further stated that, "We bring with us when we come to earth all of the collection of previous experiences and enlightenment that we have learned throughout our entire spiritual life and it is stored forever in our soul and our Light body."

Some of it is easier to consciously recall than other things. So, "depending on how we live our life on earth, and what we do with our life during the time that we have on earth, we can either learn that which we have already learned, learn in varying degrees what we came here to learn, or accomplish everything that we set out to learn by coming back here for both the teaching and learning experiences."

We gain from experiences that could only be gained while here on earth in the teaching zone. And, as John Dull stated in his book, *Everyday Lessons*, "we are either here on earth to teach, to learn, or both."

Gabe stated that when we transition from earth to the other side (where he is currently), "all learning is through enlightenment. So, when one transitions from the other side back to earth, all learning is through the experiences gained while on earth." Because life on earth is so very short (comparatively speaking to all of time, which is endless), it is hard to imagine how short the period of time on earth truly is even if one lives to be ninety or a hundred years old.

So, learning through experience is critical to the process of spiritual growth. And it is only an opportunity to be found where we are now. We either use this to grow in the Universal Spirit of God, or, we move away from this by traveling in another direction. But here on earth, there is a sense of urgency for us.

Just recently, he told me that "earth experiences are necessary, yet, they are so slow and tend to slow down the overall learning process of the soul." Still, they are necessary and cannot be avoided. A certain amount of earth learning experiences are needed to illuminate the soul. If we, as human beings don't learn what we are supposed to learn while here on earth, we will be required at some point in time to come back to learn what we failed to learn from previously. Obviously, we then slow our learning process down even further keeping us from our soulful destiny, ultimately, to become one with the Light.

In relative terms (to all of time), "time on earth is like a spec of sand on a beach full of sand," Gabe stated. I could hardly comprehend how small that period of time truly is in the overall balance of one's entire spiritual life. But it truly humbles me to think about it. It makes me want to live in the moment more and more as I consider this.

The song by Seals and Crofts, "We may never pass this way again," is a certainty. We likely will have the opportunity to return to earth, that will be a choice that we will make again,; however, we will never return under the same exact circumstances or timeframe for growing and learning in our present life.

So many other messages have come across that have had such meaning to me personally that I can only endeavor to talk about those that have had the greatest impact on me and which may have that effect on others. Some discussions of enlightenment have been seemingly insignificant to all of life in a spiritual way, but, rather interesting and fascinating to me personally. For example, during one communication, my son indicated, that "there are many, many dogs who walk the streets on the other side," where he is.

Because "they are not in a preying instinct because there is no need for food here, they get along so well that they are no threat to each other or other spirits." Subsequently, it is a more significant and harmonious relationship that those dogs have with all of creation on the other side.

I found that to be a fascinating thought. I have three dogs myself and I cannot imagine having a more wonderful relationship than I do now with any of them! Incidentally, when they pass over, if they have a conscience… they can return to you on the other side! All of them! It is by your choice, then and there.

I have always had a great appreciation for the "King of Rock," Elvis Presley. And, not long ago, I attended a premiere showing of his *1968 Jam Sessions*, which were not previously shown to the public, even though they had been recorded at the time. And so I attended this event at a cost of fifteen dollars at a local cinema theater and found it to be truly entertaining!

While there viewing this picture, I felt someone giving me an elbow to the rib cage in a very mild way and I looked to my right and heard my son say to me clearly, "Isn't this great, Dad?" For one brief moment, I imagined that he was truly there just because the sudden and unexpected reality of this, and the knowledge I had that it truly was Gabe's voice gave me the genuine sense that he was sitting right next to me enjoying it with me!

The lesson I learned from this came later that evening when I briefly spoke to Gabe through my wife, Dawn, and asked him if he had attended this concert with me. He indicated, "yeah," and that he truly was sitting on my right and that he asked me that question. This reinforced the importance of having a sense of awareness for him and how we can still do things together! This comforts me and reminds me that we all have the ability to share our life with those we love and those we refer to as "living spirits or souls"

Gabe permitted me to ask him if Elvis Presley was with him, where he is now? And he indicated, "Elvis is here. However, he is quite busy. He still performs, and there are so many souls who line up to see him each day that I don't have the desire to wait in line to meet him. However, if I chose to, I could."

He went on to talk about the fact that many celebrities such as Elvis who transitioned to that side still perform, but the reason so many souls want to meet them or be with them is because of the many unusual and different experiences that they had while they were living on earth. What can be learned from those experiences by all souls can grant enlightenment from having those souls share the messages from the experiences and what they learned from them while on earth.

Another interesting lesson that I gave great consideration to was that he indicated that in transitioning to his side (afterlife), there was a remarkable beauty that was so significantly awesome that it was greater than anything we can know here on earth! "It is virtually indescribable at times." Gabe said. The extraordinary illumination of colors that are used wherever one looks places a surreal feeling around every object.

He also has indicated that the shimmering Light that all souls glow in, due to the concentration of vibration and the level of vibration that they live in at their frequency, creates beauty and understanding for all to recognize.

He has indicated in his earliest communications to us that all music that comes to the earth emanates from his level at that time (level four). It emanates "through vibrations sent by angels that herald at all times." The vibrations then form different vibrations as they pass through frequency waves, and we, as humans, interpret those vibrations and develop our own sense of music from what we believe to be the sounds that we feel, sense, and hear that radiate from our souls. In fact, the inspiration for the music we make is given to us by choirs of angels from the afterlife.

In some our earlier communications, Gabe said that the music was magnificent and that he could "tune it in or tune it out whenever he chose to, but that it was beautiful to have all the same." He also indicated in a later communications that really all things can be tuned in and tuned out by him whenever it is necessary.

In the afterlife, depending on your vibration levels and Light illumination, (soul evolvement), you simply manifest anything and everything that you choose to by mental transference (telepathic communication).

He mentioned that he does attend a lot of educational programming at the level where he is. It is always available at all times. So much learning occurs in afterlife, in what we would consider a short period of time (from an earth-time-continuum standpoint), and yet, there is so much to be learned and so many different types of classes that one can involve himself in.

It is a perpetual process that one wants to be a part of voluntarily. To continue to move forward in the process of spiritual development there, Gabe participates in classes constantly for his enjoyment and personal-growth process. He stated that "it is necessary at times for him to have such intensity with his learning that he has to tune everything else out in order to have the right amount of solitude to absorb all of the literal aspects of what he is learning."

One of the classes that he took early on was the literal interpretation of all of the messages that Jesus gave while he was on earth. This meant "word for word," and "phrase by phrase," and he studied what the true and accurate meaning of each of those intended messages were, as it was necessary for him to have that information to be able to evolve to a higher level and to teach others. I asked him who taught the class and he said, "the actual people (spirits) who were closest to Jesus and present at the times that he spoke His words."

Gabe is in awe of the amount of education that is available at all times there. Whatever you want or need to comprehend, you simply place yourself in that class. Another interesting fact that he brought to our attention in a different communications was when he discussed "Jesus" with me. I asked him if "he had ever spoken to Jesus?" And he replied, "yes." However, he went on to state that "Jesus is quite busy, Dad. He keeps a pretty active schedule."

Not long ago when I was essentially sharing information with him, (he called it something else), I asked him if he had spoken to Jesus recently. His immediate reply was, "Dad, you have been monopolizing so much of his time lately that I can't get in to see him!"

I momentarily lost it (cracking up), because the thought of Jesus being too busy to see Gabe was probably the funniest thought that my mind had imagined in some time. I pictured him with a day runner, looking it over closely, wondering when he could squeeze "Gabe Vaught in for a personal greeting."

Gabe's sense of humor is still very apparent to us. I asked him at an earlier discussion, "Gabe, how do you think Jesus would feel if, when I transitioned to the afterlife, I simply followed him around wherever he went?" Gabe pondered the questioned carefully, then stated, "Frankly, Dad, I think he would be scared to death!" God, I laughed until tears were rolling down my smile.

Gabe went on to educate me by saying that "Jesus actually has the ability to move between any and all levels of life as he so chooses, when he so chooses." There are no limitations on Jesus, and He can be anywhere and everywhere at the same time. This meant that in the eleven levels of life that Gabe had described to us that existed to his knowledge at that time, God is at level eleven, and Gabe is at level four, Jesus actually moves to and about all levels to gain insight and understanding and share and teach at each and all levels.

In the afterlife, they don't actually refer to ascension or descension as it would reflect a connotative description of something more or less. They don't use those types of measurements in the afterlife. You either move toward the Light or away from it.

I did ask Gabe early on, perhaps, before he knew there were informational transfer boundaries there, if he knew whether Jesus has ever returned to the earth following his resurrection. His reply really surprised me. He stated, "Jesus has returned many, many times. He comes and He goes, according to the needs of some. He comes unannounced and leaves that way, as a rule."

Although I have seldom discussed the eleven levels of afterlife existence to this point in any great detail with Gabriel, yet, I have learned that level four is a level where we learn to be more accepting, more loving, and more peaceful with all of God's creation. Each level is the complete essence of the level before it, he stated. It is a purer state of the previous state of living.

Gabe has stated that so many concepts of enlightenment in the afterlife exist, that we have no understanding or comprehension of most of them here on earth. The same is true with words that we are not familiar with and thoughts that we are not familiar with, yet are used there.

Because it is so difficult to compare the earthly sense of urgency and space-time continuum to the fact that there is no time continuum where he lives, he tries to translate into earthly years what we can expect as we look ahead and try to place some understanding on the time table for developments or events which will occur. But the relevance of time here and there really has no comparison.

One day, he indicated to me that he was sitting on a very extraordinary committee of great thinkers who are working now on a plan to bring "world peace to the earth." I could not resist in asking him how soon that might occur? After a great pause, he indicated that their hope was that they could complete "the peace plan" and deliver on the execution of that "peace plan" on earth in approximately fifty thousand earth years.

I told him "can you imagine what it would be like for the world to continue on as it is now for another fifty thousand years before seeing significant progress?"

"It can all change in the blink of an eye, Dad. The total energy that radiates from all living souls on earth will determine the earth's fate. If people don't become consciously aware of how powerful each individual's energy really is, and how they must learn to use it, there will be little chance for change. Yet, if one person could reach everyone else and grant them the understanding of what collective consciousness really means in living in the Light of God, the world would instantly change in a heartbeat. "It is each soul that will determine the earth's fate, Dad!"

I have since learned that, although Gabe made no mention of this to me, there is an approximate date of fifty thousand earth years when the Second Coming of Jesus has been forecasted by a "knowledgeable afterlife soul." Because I only received this in a transmission from a spiritual afterlife teacher in an educational class that I attended, I am not prepared to comment on the possible correlation that these two events might have together.

I was told by this teacher, (who is and was world renown for practicing non-violent peace measures above all else), that for those who will come with Jesus for The Second Coming, it is like they should be packing their bags now (in figurative terms).

Time is that short in all of existence by their frame of reference and for eternal living. While this is a figurative form of speaking, they are in soulful preparation for the Second Coming now, though, I have learned.

Perhaps the greatest message that I have received that meant something to me on a personal level between my son and I was one that I will share with you that involves our being together now and forever more. From day one when he initially talked with us and communicated what he wanted us to know early on about his passing, I have been concerned about whether I would ever see him again in the sense of how we saw him here, physically, as our son.

He put that to rest by saying there were many ways we could continue to be together now during the time that we live in different transition forms of energy, however, we would always be together, forever. At first, I concerned myself that that was a very euphoric comment meaning that in our hearts and our minds we would always think of one another throughout our eternal lives. But he has made it a point on many occasions to clarify that by saying that he will be there to meet me when I transition from earth to his side and that we will be together forever more, as we choose to be. In the meantime, we will spend many happy and joyous celebrations of life together. He can be here whenever I call, or whenever he chooses to join us.

I am encouraged by that thought and it is really what motivated me so often each day when only eight weeks after his burial I was still suffering so much pain, emotionally and psychologically, adjusting to life here on earth without him, physically, and yet reveling in his messages of inspiration to me.

I recognize that life must go on here and there are many lessons that I must still learn before I can make my transition to the other side. "All things in their own time" is how I best think of this.

"I am with you now and we are inseparable." This was a line from a letter that I had written to Gabe before his death.

Just very recently, he indicated to me that my father will be passing away before long in his relatively short remaining life here, so Gabe said that he will be there before he passes away. During the time he is passing and transitioning to the other side and then, forever more, Gabe and Grandpa Vaught will share life together. That has to be tremendous news for Grandpa Vaught! He thinks of Gabe in the same way that I do...as one of his own! I am so comforted to know that the person I love so much, who has taught me so much as my father here on earth, will be with the other person I love so much who has also been a living inspiration for me, and my son here on earth.

Gabe has told me that we both lived before together in the *Byzantine era*, roughly twelve hundred years before Christ was born to the earth. At that time, he indicated, we were best friends and fought together to the end.

He further stated that there has always been conflict in the world because man knows not how to think clearly when given the opportunity to negotiate a better solution, while having the desire to demonstrate man's muscle (power). If man had considered the earth and all of its inhabitants as sacred, how many wars would have been fought over trivial differences?

So, I wonder aloud, since God created the earth, is it not sacred?

But what made me even happier is that my son went on to say that we'll all three (my father now, my son, and I) will all be together again forever more. It has been decided and it is certain. I can't tell you how much this means to know that my father and my son want to spend their eternal lives with me! My love and affection for those two is so great! It will be a reality that I look forward to throughout my remaining life on earth, for all of us.

The only questionable concern that has been raised in our communications in talking with our son thus far is the fact that he indicated he could easily read my future because I permit him to and have agreed in contract form before I came to the earth to permit him to read my thoughts at all times.

Still, he indicated the same is not true with his mother, my wife, Dawn. Therefore, he cannot read her future, and as a result, is unable to tell me much about her in our conversations other than what he observes from the hereafter, now.

I had asked if there was a probability that she, too, would spend eternal life with us, and he indicated that he did not know. While I realize that there are no guarantees with any of this because so much of it is a puzzle that we cannot piece together while still living here, it does concern me that the person whom I love so dearly now, and who has meant so much to my life here on earth, might not be a part of my eternal life, hereafter. Perhaps it is a lesson to all of us to remember that we shall take nothing, and no one, for granted in our lifetime.

Each day, each person we see or we meet, is special! In that I have heard it said before, I shall quote this passage without giving credit to its rightful states person, though I acknowledge them as brilliant: "You may only be one person to the world, but you may mean the world to one person." Somehow, I believe that is a deep-seated truth for all of mankind to remember.

I choose to believe that there is a plan that we've all agreed to it in one form or another. And, it is God's will that we determine what is best for our eternal life development. Perhaps, we are just caring souls facilitating one another's development for this lifetime, and beyond. That would make each of us caretakers of our brethren. Perhaps that is how we come to a greater understanding of God and our personal Light prospects.

I have not yet discussed with him the issue of converging pathways meeting, what the lessons of the timing of those are, and how we are impacted in different ways. But in time, I hope to understand that better and pass that information along. It is like so many things that come about through time, though, perhaps it is best to let time answer those questions for each of us. I can only think of so many things at once that I want to hear and communicate to my son about, and through the first eight weeks, I felt like we made great progress. Since then, we have astounded my wife, my friends, and those who cannot fully comprehend these communications. I have been astounded by the importance of the enlightenment that has been shared for all of us to learn from, especially me. I was without a clue as to so many of these dynamics that are just one element or part of God's plan for us.

My purpose for recording certain information immediately, and to the degree that was possible, was to attempt to save the true meaning and interpretations of all of the information as best as I could at that given moment. The messages are so meaningful to my life in bringing more peace and comfort since Gabe's transition from the earth.

It has been less comforting to my wife because she cannot retain much, if any, of the messages without listening to the recordings. So therefore, it is laborious to a degree and difficult because of the amount of energy it takes for her to transmit this energy through the channeling process. There is (to a degree) less of the immediate rewards in hearing our son speak to us. But she does this out of the goodness of her heart because she sees what it does for me, and how one more soul headed in God's direction can mean many positive events for others that I come into contact with daily.

Because of this…she takes my lessons for learning from all of this to a whole new level for me. She teaches me the real value of loving unconditionally and caring so deeply for someone that she gives of herself freely and without hesitation, mostly for my benefit. I love her so much and share that she, too, is an inspiration to me!

My wife has always shown this to me throughout my life and it has heightened my love for her and others because I see what a shining example of unconditional love truly looks like firsthand. I am so fortunate to have her close to me! This was no accident, I am certain.

Every turn now I am dedicating my life to looking for ways to fulfill her every need to the best that I can by assisting her in finding her own objectives, her own goals, and her own desires through her discovery process on earth this time. I am blessed with her spirit.

All that remains in my mind from the questions that are still raised from the conversations that are ongoing with our son at this time are, "what will we do with this information as we move on in our lives, and how will we make the most of our opportunity to fulfill our destinies and our learning experiences that still remain in the years that lie ahead for Dawn and I?"

All human beings have that question to face before we transition to the other side, but for me, this is a very personal matter and one that takes a great deal of effort to share at this time.

I know that certain conscious souls in this world who choose to believe will have insight in to what I am experiencing and what my family has been experiencing in the most intimate way through these revelations of my life. Still, my hope is that the educational service (the planting of seeds) that this book can provide can begin to outline for others the opportunities and experiences that potentially lie ahead for each of us while we are still here on earth.

We can learn to examine what we believe in and then choose to believe in things that we have not previously learned, but that are presented to us to learn from what we have to look forward to hereafter, obviously. The greatest lesson any of us can learn seems to be that whatever we give our beliefs to will provide energy that, when set into motion, will create the perceived rewards or consequences of our quality of life here. If we learn better from "suffering," then we should choose "suffering" as our objective for this life. And, if we learn better from physical or mental or emotional challenges, then so be it. We have then what we need to grow from.

I have a friend who has no problem believing that if he invests ten million dollars (physical world) in a condominium project in the right location for him, he will earn many millions of dollars over and above his investment. He places his faith and trust in this thought process, and then gives it energy as he works toward that outcome at completion of the project. Yet, he struggles with the same thinking process when it comes to dedicating his growth and awareness through discovery of the afterlife and the messages and purpose for these communications. Why? Why does he hold doubt for the spiritual investment and accept the physical plane of existence for himself?

His lessons must revolve around the physical challenges of his life. Perhaps, he was quite poor at one time and had elected to overcome this condition for the learning experience it provides.

Yet, why can he trust his instincts, but not those of God, who places this information in front of him through me? He sees me as the provider of the information, and not simply the messenger or courier that I am. Because of this, he doubts my statements to a degree and whether or not I have what I say that I have (meaning, an intimate expression of love for Christ, the Holy Spirit, and God, by delivering their messages to this world.

God needs various communicators. Some through nature, some through living souls here on earth, and some through the divinely guided in the hereafter. More people believe in angels now than ever before in the recorded history of earth. Why?

Gabe's dress wear for his prom night during his Sophomore year in HS

Gabe and friend Robbie "takin it easy" at Robbie's family vacation in Gulf Shores AL

CHAPTER NINE

Fulfilling My Destiny — Changing My Spiritual Journey

Before my son passed away, I must say that if I were asked to describe what I believed my spiritual journey to be here on earth was, it would have been one of *charity* for the most part.

In an early conversation with our son (shortly after he passed away), he confirmed that both my wife and I had spent the first half of our lives doing just that, being charitable, and now it was time for us to learn new lessons that were to be charted by us through new experiences, new friendships, and new passageways to spiritual enlightenment and development.

I had always thought of myself, due to my ability to find sufficient resources for myself when they were needed, and for helping others in their time of need, as the "provider" when others were without those things that were critical to their lives. Particularly my family, but many times, complete strangers to whom I had a heartfelt sense of obligation during any sort of crisis of which I became knowledgeable with them.

I remember one Christmas, my wife and I heard about a family that had been burned out of their home in Lafayette, Indiana, and had to relocate to a vacant home in nearby Frankfort, Indiana, two days before Christmas. They had eight children, supported by a single mother with no child support, and no visible means of income, and no other assistance at that time.

I first heard about their home going up in flames on a local/regional television station that I seldom ever watched, up to that day. My first thought was that surely a certain number of people will pitch in to help! Still, something tugged at my vest and told me not to count on that and to take the lead and make certain that the children and the family had a "very special Christmas to celebrate."

My wife and I purchased more than a thousand dollars' worth of gifts, toys, groceries, and necessary hygiene products, and drove to Frankfort, Indiana, and investigated their whereabouts until we could locate them living in a vacant home there that someone had been kind enough to donate for temporary housing for them.

We surprised them by showing up on their doorstep to introduce ourselves on Christmas Eve at about 3:00 PM. We proceeded to make many trips back and forth from the van to deliver all of the goods to them. It was such a satisfying and deeply rewarding moment for all of us to watch the faces of those children as we brought food, toys, surprises, and candy to them that day! To this day, I still think that we were the people who benefited most from that experience, and not necessarily the family we helped at that time. The kids loved it all, but we took the "spirit of Christmas" back home with us and our hearts felt warmer than ever before that year.

That was a wonderful gift to give to ourselves! And the family that we helped had hope again, and a "dream come true, if only for awhile."

The same thing happened one other Christmas Eve, when we had selected the family of a prisoner to take Christmas to and learned, when we delivered those gifts on Christmas Eve that the family had sadly been evicted from their property the previous day. With nowhere to go, we drove around on Christmas Eve until we found a nearby fire station in close proximity to where we lived.

We walked in at 8:00 PM to ask if there was anyone in need of children's clothing and/or gifts for Christmas. The fireman looked at us (astonished to some degree) and said, "why yes, there was a family who lost their entire home earlier today and are without anything for Christmas and I can assure you these gifts would be much appreciated." God had a plan. We simply had to follow our hearts and be guided to the place we needed to be.

In each case, I felt as though this was God's will, and our desires to fulfill God's will, and we were fulfilling our destiny by carrying out these random acts of kindness. We were being guided to do what we were here to do, which was to act as an instrument of charity in these situations. However, we were the blessed!

There were many other occasions where we helped loved ones and others, but these two highlight for me the opportunities that I had to help complete strangers that I will never know (Strangers who belong to the same family that I do...the human family).

Yet, today, it is apparently time for me to learn from new experiences and therefore, I sit and ponder the notion of what those experiences should be, and where I might be guided to, to put myself in the most appropriate place and location to begin a new learning process now.

I was reminded very recently in communications with my son that it is best to allow the experiences to come to me by stepping into the "flow of life," rather than seeking the "flow of life," at all times. It is possible while seeking the "flow of life," to miss it altogether, he indicated. While going about your business, it will be easy for the flow of life to find you. Particularly if you're aware and consciously able to see it coming as you relate to your needs and the lessons you are to learn with the opportunities that present themselves.

I took this to mean that I can be anywhere and still find the "*right opportunities*" that I'm supposed to find as I look forward to learning from new experiences that will help my spiritual development in the days that lie ahead.

One other reminder that came from my son most recently is that worrying and being stressed out due to conscious or subconscious anxiety will seriously diminish the ability to function properly and to be able to step into the "flow of life" and remain there consistently.

He indicated that "*so much energy is required in worrying and being stressed that it prevents us from seeing the opportunities, let alone consciously executing them at the appropriate, opportune times.*"

He further explained that worrying and anxiety create mental, spiritual, and emotional drains that are not only useless, but meaningless, to our spiritual development. Because God knows our needs, and we have a contract to fulfill regarding our spiritual destiny, we need only to continue on in being the best that we can be each moment of each day and allow "the flow of life" to find us. Anything else is irrelevant and mindless activity and really unnecessary for us to concern ourselves with.

So, I'm doing a lot less worrying these days and my results are so much better! But the truth is, it's an unusual pattern for me. I have always concerned myself about being the primary provider for our family financially, as well as the strength and courage and stability for our family emotionally during times of crisis. I'm not sure that I need to be any or all of those things anymore. Subsequently, I'm practicing very progressive consideration in giving all of that up. Not because I feel the need to do nothing, but because I no longer feel the need to hold onto those things that I thought gave me some type of control in the past over my life. We have a say so in our life. We do not have the only say so in our life. We also have divine intervention.

I believe that God will lead me where he wants me, when he calls upon me, and I believe that my son will help communicate with me where he believes I may need to grow at any given time when I lack clarity with this. This is the beauty of allowing the afterlife to guide you and assist you at times!

As a worst-case scenario, my soul will gently remind me when I have strayed off track. I just have to be willing to listen to that inner voice that speaks to me not in a human voice tone, but in a God-centered, feeling, voice transmission through my heart and soul.

I have been prepared on two occasions by two completely different people that there is a very good likelihood that at some point in time, all communications will cease with my son as he moves on to future challenging responsibilities that he has with his own spiritual development. From a rational standpoint, I could understand this and accept it. From a very emotional standpoint, I pray that this will not happen any time soon as I am enjoying getting to know him better, learning through his wisdom and light, and hearing his expressions and the resilience of his cadence through my wife's voice and just knowing that he is still with us. He observes and takes part in the many earthly experiences that my wife and I still share each day.

It brings me great satisfaction and comfort to believe that he can participate with us even though he isn't physically here any longer, because I know his heart and soul are with us wherever we may go.

I feel them and his presence so much of the time now.

Still, if the time comes when my son must move on, then I will know that this too is a necessary part of the plan. In Dan Fogelberg's hit song from the seventies, "Part of the Plan," there are words that say "await your arrival, simple survival, and one day, we'll all understand....one day we'll all understand." More than anything else, I have become a believer that if I am to step into the "flow of life" consistently, I need to realize that my immediate desires and expectations are only a small part of what my life is all about. And one day, I'll better understand, no doubt.

My major life goals now are to fulfill God's will by instituting a more God-centered will for myself and living in the Spirit of Jesus Christ as consistently as I can. Forever more, I want to fulfill my destiny by being everything that I set out to be here on earth. If I am to be...it is up to me! Through His guidance and my faith and my will!

This seems to be a major development in my spiritual journey and one that I will always be grateful for as it feels better, seems better, and seems right in how I feel about it and am experiencing it. "I'm going with the flow!"

Giving up control has never been easy for me as I have always used control as a means by which to feel as though I am valuable to myself and of value to others. At the same time, that is such a selfish and limited role and such a limited perspective on life that it's a wonder that I haven't diminished my educational experiences to a large degree by assuming that mental picture for so much of my life.

For one to seek control as a means of gaining an advantage over one's life (or even another person's life), seems to me to be "stepping outside the flow of life" to a large degree and acting in a manner that is out of control. Leave it to God! Just do your thing and be certain it is kind, just, loving, considerate, and of value to you and/or to others.

I don't believe that this means that you have to give up your desires or your goals or your objectives in life, it just means that there is a time and place for all things. I have learned that assertiveness does not need to occur twenty-four hours a day, seven days a week, three hundred and sixty-five days a year for me to be able to enjoy my life in a way that achieves great results and accomplishments for those things that I am actively pursuing.

I'm working on understanding the need for assertiveness and when it is best to use — and advocating it to be used by others where I once used it too often for my own good.

In this way, I gain new perspectives and develop new understanding of what life is all about by seeing life through an enhanced picture frame that takes into consideration many other possibilities of thinking, other than strictly assuming a desired posture of taking, and being in control at all times.

In a counseling session that my wife and I attended one week together, I heard her say something that was profoundly educational to me when she indicated to the counselor (and myself) that her goal at this point in time is to simply return to the level of spirituality that she had prior to the time that our son passed away from earth.

I thought about the true meaning of that, because my wife has always been a deeply spiritual person. It occurred to me that some people are here at a level that is so elevated early on in their life, that their life experiences — their wisdom, their God given knowledge (even though they continue to live on earth and gain experiences that they need for whatever their purposes may be) — are totally different than mine.

They have achieved a level that they want to be at for a significantly longer period of time than others, perhaps. Their lessons are not our lessons, necessarily. So, how can we judge anyone at all?

I should be so lucky as to have the spiritual forces and guidance that my wife has had throughout her life here on earth. She has been one of the main reasons that I began to examine my life at such an early age while still in my twenties.

I have thought many times about how blessed I am to have been surrounded by so many angels here on earth, literally and figuratively. Now that my son has passed away and I've had time to reflect on this further, I believe that applies to every day of my life.

It is always difficult to know how precious anything is until the absence of that blessing occurs. In the matter of my wife, I have known all along that she was here to guide not only her life through the experiences that were necessary for her learning purposes, but to help me to achieve mine as well. I am so deeply grateful for what she has been able to teach me through her guidance. Many times she just laughs at me when I tell her these things. I think she thinks that I am patronizing her because I want something, perhaps. Often, I thank her at the most unusual times. When in fact, I just don't ever want there to be a misunderstanding about how much or how often I acknowledge what her life has meant to mine. It is deeply important to me that she knows that she has been the most influential person that I have ever met here on earth. My son is right there with her as well. Add my son, Noah, and I have had incredible teachers and guides to live my life with here on earth.

I have intentionally left out much of the discussion about my family in this book for purposes of maintaining their rights to their personal experiences, attachments, and sorrow over this deeply sad experience with the physical death of Gabe, and dealing with their own sadness and belief systems.

In no way are they experiencing this whirlwind of tragedy nearly as enthusiastically as I am, when it comes to looking at the larger picture of what this whole experience means to our lives. How could they? They haven't had these same experiences to influence them! However, I have had some level of communications with all of them about what their lives have been like here on earth, and what they still expect from life, and what Gabriel has told us to some degree about what they can expect hereafter.

I've been so surprised by the level of interest that some family members have shown to me in wanting to learn more about this experience, and using this information to bring more happiness to their life each day.

In whatever time that they may have left while still here on earth, they can see life for more of what it is and less of what it seems to be from a distance (rather than introspectively seeking the inward path to God).

Since so many people are so afraid of the unknown and the uncertainty of the hereafter, it is hard to know who to discuss subjects like this with openly and in person. I'm so grateful to my parents for allowing me to do this and it is just one more reason why I've always felt I could talk to my parents about anything.

Other family members find the subject to be "taboo". I cannot relate as well to that thinking , however, I can respect it. *We are all in different places, spaces, and time, with our journeys.*

Now my father is eighty-three years young, and in relatively good health, although his years are numbered (just like us all)! My mother is seventy-nine and the same could be said for her. Still, they care enough to listen and they care enough to ask questions and I truly believe this experience will have impacted them in a very positive way as they prepare for their time when they too will transition to be with my son, once again.

The sweet result of conferring with afterlife spirits is that we grow to better understand them, love them, respect them, and fear not at all what lays ahead for each of us. We are visiting this earth. Our home is not in Alabama…but in a place I think of as true paradise, God's place for us, where eternal life continues.

The spiritual journey still has much definition left and I still have much to learn from the days that lie ahead. It is my hope that in these days that lie ahead that I will continue to grow closer to stepping into the "flow of life" through the many windows of opportunity that present themselves to me. While I still can talk with Gabe about anything and everything, he is quick to remind me that there are others I can speak with too, on earth and in heaven.

Not long ago, I asked him if he would contact Jesus for me and ask Him something on my behalf? He said, "Dad, you ask Him. I'm your son, not your messenger!" He went on to say, "Jesus's only job is to be here for all people who need Him and want Him and ask for Him." Just reach out for Him and he will answer you. Whether you hear His answer will depend on what you are willing to hear.

It is through the course of these incredible communications that I have learned that life is much deeper and much more meaningful when it is examined more fully. This I have begun to do. I would recommend it for everyone, no matter what age you may be. It is never too late to contact these living souls. One day, you will be one and I feel certain you will want someone to contact you from earth. Perhaps, we will have made this possible by then through the understanding that this book and others with similar messages can offer.

We are not separate living souls. For real life has no separation, no beginning, and no end! We are one in God's spirit and energy. Why must we separate ourselves with concerns for black or white, good or bad, rich or poor? We are all together in this eternal life. Let's stop pretending that we are not. What matters to one of us truly affects all of us.

I suggest that we quit pretending that we don't know or can't accept each other. We came from one and we are one...even with those we hold in contempt. For as brave and as valiant as our notions may seem, who among us shall cast the first stone?

Two of Gabe's very favorite women in the entire world – Aunt Donna   and Mammaw Vaught (taken at the annual race day celebration in Carmel, IN)

Gabe and Dad celebrating one last time at the Pumpkin Patch near Noblesville, IN , near Halloween (a family tradition that began even before Gabe was even born and celebrated each and every year thereafter until it closed Gabe's Senior year)

CHAPTER TEN

Sharing My Feelings before He Transitioned

> *"'Oh Lord, our father…be thou near them' and 'Help us tear their soldiers to bloody shreds,' expresses man's hypocrisy by showing that while we do not want to risk our own, we expect to destroy the opponent."*

I found this among hundreds and hundreds of papers my son had written throughout his formal educational journey here on earth. This happened to be one from Ms. Konare's English class G4 written on April 22, 2002 — two years and one day before he passed away from earth. On that same page of writing, I discovered the following expressions that were obvious to me to be homework assignments that Gabe had completed in English after reading a specific assignment, but the answers by themselves were all that appeared on this page.

I continued to read.

> *"The aged man is an emissary of God. Not only do his words make sense and have great meaning, but to oppose such a large crowd with such confidence would take more than madness… it would take divine reassurance.*

"Victory is always double-edged. Every event in the world is double-edged. Newton's Law states that every action has an equal and opposite reaction. Also, in my personal experience, I have never experienced anything that had all rewards while lacking consequences. Even the most pure emotion, love, can cause pain and suffering. This is why victory must be double-edged."

I found this information in Gabe's dormitory room the day after he had passed on. I held onto it like it was the most precious information that I had ever come across in my life. Because at that moment, that's what it seemed like to me. What I felt inside was that my son had experienced how to use not only his extraordinary intellect, but much of his wisdom gained throughout the early and formidable years of his young life.

My heart smiled to think that he had truly listened many times during our most stimulating conversations to my point of view, and other's point of view, as well. I was always sharing with him *the other side of the coin. I wanted him to think as he would want to be thought about.*

I had hoped that he would be capable of examining his feelings and others feelings, too, before making up his mind how to reference any information that came unto him.

I was forever providing him information to help equip and prepare him for how to manage the most difficult encounters of his life. Many times, I did so with clichés, as I felt they were easier to recall on a moment's notice than some long, complex formula of patterns and elements that would require too much thought for the spur of the moment. Besides, I knew I would have a hard time keeping his attention if I didn't make it short and sweet in summary form, customarily.

The point is that he learned at such an early age to share his true feelings while also being able to express his intellect at the same time, and still giving others the benefit of expressing themselves. I've always felt this was the strength of a great communicator, writer, messenger, and leader. And I felt that throughout his lifetime, he had worked extremely hard to characterize himself in ways that truly expressed his point of view without offending others. He could let people see different sides of his personality, his understanding, his compassion for all others, and his immense wisdom that were uncharacteristic of kids his age, as a rule. He maintained an "old soul" emotional appearance, making him an interesting ambassador of goodwill to others. It would be fair to say that he was an unconventional "diplomat for peace here on earth, and goodwill toward men."

Two years before Gabe passed away, I had already begun grieving for reasons that I did not fully understand then. I spent many nights crying alone. I took many lonely walks by myself and would cry and sob and the only rational means I had of understanding what was happening was to believe that I was perhaps, somehow, experiencing a physical, chemical form of depression as a result of my diabetes. And, I may have been doing just that.

Yet, my grief was always the same and always revolved around my son, Gabriel. It was as if I perceived he was going away too soon!

It wasn't until several days after Gabriel had passed away and I received an extraordinary communications from him from the other side, saying that he could explain why I grieved so much and why I had a sense of discomfort for so long prior to his passing.

Here is a letter that was written approximately thirty days before Gabriel transitioned from physical form here on this earth to his spiritual life form now. These are actual documented letters that I felt compelled to write to him to attempt to explain my inner feelings at a time when I could not fully understand them at all. I actually placed titles in letters to him, as though they were poems or presentations of some nature.

This one I titled "As a Father ...I've Learned that Goodbye Is not Forever"

Gabriel,

Once again, I am so very proud of you and the many accomplishments that you are bringing to your life each and every day. Your mother and I marvel at how great your judgment and decision-making skills are, now that you are living on your own. We also pray for you so that, if and when difficult decisions must be made by you, that you will have spiritual reinforcement and the will of those you love to lean on.

Still, I confess that each time we must part for undetermined periods of time, I sense a great loss. I know that you will come back and I will come to see you. And in between, we will talk or write as we feel the need to. At the same time, only a father or mother can appreciate how difficult it is to say goodbye when we are not certain how much opportunity that we will have to see you, be with you, and simply share our love with our child... even though you are eighteen years old and a growing adult now.

So, we trust and we hope beyond hope that our parenting skills taught you some of what you need to know to understand that you are never alone. We are with you every day in spirit and in our deep devotion to you in all ways. We recognize how far you have traveled to take advantage of the opportunities that you have now. You need them, you deserve them, and you'll come to cherish them as a part of a growth and evolutionary process that will ultimately bring you to a very satisfying and happy place in your heart, if it isn't already feeling that way now.

Time flies by, and yet, it can seem to take forever when you are anticipating something that has not occurred yet, but that you are looking forward to.....such as goals and dreams. Growth and development are what occur while you are traveling toward your goals and dreams. And when you get sidetracked (and we all do on occasions), you are still on the right path. Sometimes, it may not feel like it, but trust me when I tell you that unless you are doing something to bring harm to yourself or others, you are always on the right path. Every path has a different result and, sometimes, different paths converge when you least expect them to. And your results are the combination of your will, your actions, and your sacrifices.

The fact that we know these things brings to us great comfort and allows us to say goodbye to you with a smile in our hearts...even if our faces don't reflect this. We know that our "faith" is what carries us when we have an absence of knowledge. For it is all there is if one believes in the power of positive thinking. I do, and I believe that we never walk alone. My belief is that God is with us at all times.

So, I've learned that goodbye is not forever. It is a temporary way of choosing to part ways physically for me. I never part ways spiritually, mentally, or emotionally with you, and I never will. The day that I no longer live here on earth in physical form will only be the next day of my life. You will be a part of me here and hereafter. We are inseparable. Sometimes when we pretend to have problems with each other (or it seems as though we really do), I think it is our emotional conscience preparing us for the next departure and saying to us "let me help you make it easier to say goodbye this time."

With every day that you live, remember these things and know that we'll always support you and love you as you grow up and on. Even if we can't be with you, we will be. Please think of us in this way and it will be easier for you to do the things that your life calls you to do, also.

We have different destinies, we are different people, tied by the Almighty power of love, faith, and family. These bonds never permit a final separation. Our hearts are one with you....forever.

Trust your heart and use your head and you will fly free to every destination that you want for yourself throughout your life here on earth. It is a right of passage for those that care to have and

make sacrifices for their own happiness. Goodbye, son…make
each day special!

With all my love for you. May God Bless and keep you safe.

Dad

When I went back and read this letter (about three days after he had passed away), I realized how prophetic it was in virtually every word and sentence of it. It seemed too coincidental to be able to write these feelings to him just thirty days before the time that he passed away, knowing that each and every one of those words might have just as easily been spoken or written by him, to me.

And then the communications from my son several days after he passed away revealed what I did not know before. He told me this, "Dad, before I ever came to the earth, we agreed by contract that I would live a certain number of days and hours upon the earth and fulfill certain lessons that I had to learn there in order to gain from my life experiences on earth. We all agreed to this, you, Mom, and me. And although most human beings do not remember in their conscious minds these contract agreements when they transition back to earth again, your higher consciousness permitted your subconscious mind to begin to realize the terms of this contract years before I passed away. As a result, you were able to start the grieving process and actually work your way through much of your sadness over my physical departure, Dad, before I ever passed away.

This seems remarkable to me, because even though it had to be an understandably difficult and confusing time for you, it also helped you tremendously during my sudden transition from earth to have the necessary strength, faith, and trust, that I was where I was meant to be.

"Unfortunately, Mother did not remember our contract, consciously or subconsciously, and has suffered tremendously from her loss which she perceives to be not only so sudden and unexpected, but so tragic and unexplainable now. Dad, you have to be there for Mom now and support her in ways that will help her now and long into the future. She needs your understanding and patience because she is going to have a much longer process by which she will need to grieve to overcome her extreme despair and depression from this.

"Though I understand that you'll still be grieving to an extent, I'll be there for both you and Mother in every way that I can throughout your lives on earth. However, it is the physical loss that mother is experiencing the greatest grief over at this time. So, you can physically be there for her to comfort her for me as well. I will hold her and kiss her and touch her many times and do all that I can to touch her heart to help her heal and it is still the way of mankind to grieve when someone passes from the earth. So I understand this process, yet, it truly saddens me to see both you and Mother cry and to be so sad over my passing. Because of this, I, too, cry many times when I see your tears. You see, I can also feel and experience the same things that you are feeling and experiencing while you experience them on earth.

"But you have much work to do, Dad, and many days ahead of you on earth, even though in a relative sense, it's still a short period of time. Your work will provide you with much happiness and joy throughout the years and I will look after you and be with you throughout all of this. Still, you need to keep focused on your spiritual growth and development and use your gifts, Dad, now as a human being treating the world as Gary Vaught, not so much as the father of Gabriel Vaught.

"In other words, be yourself, Dad. That's where all your strengths lie. Just be yourself. You'll always be my father and that will not change. But you are better off being who you are now and not just a parent figure. You are free to pursue your dreams and destiny."

I realized, after all his comments, that his words were not only totally selfless, but true. They brought a sense of relief and confidence to me that I had not wasted those years grieving unnecessarily or prematurely for no reason. It was a force within me that knew what was about to happen whether I consciously could have ever understood the process or not.

The letters I'm about share with you now are only a small number of letters that I wrote to Gabe before his passing, but here is one that was written on April 30, 2002.

> *Dear Gabe,*
> *I wanted to take a few moments today to tell you in written words what I have not been able to in recent days about my thoughts and feelings at this time in our lives. First, I want to say how proud your mother and I are of you for setting the example of realizing your potential as a loving son and an accomplished student. Your greatest sacrifices in your life teach you more down the road a ways than you could ever know or learn from why you are making them and experiencing them at the moment.*
>
> *Your decisions about how you want to live your life set up your entire life as you pass from day to day, week to week, and year to year. One day, you awaken to find that your efforts have either helped you to realize a good life and perhaps your goals and dreams, or something less than you had hoped for. When you awaken and discover those realities for yourself, you then better understand why you made the decisions that you did and their real meaning and value to your life.*
>
> *Secondly, the days are passing quickly now. Our time together is precious. Though so much of my time is consumed by my requirements at work, I think about you so much. I recall your smile, your laugh, your sense of humor, your straightforwardness*

and honesty, and think how lucky we are to have someone with your remarkable character and charms.

As the next year unfolds and we have new experiences and changes that we encounter in our lives together, let's remember how important we are to one another and each other. Let's keep the little things little and work on helping one another with the big things, so that we all enjoy them more and realize a bond by sticking together as a family. We are all here not just for ourselves, but for one another, too.

In some ways, these past several months to a year have been bittersweet for me. Bitter, in that I have lost valuable time to spend with you and your mother. Sweet, in that I have proven to myself once again that I can accomplish anything that I set my mind to, no matter how small or large the challenge may be.

The pizza business is just a name for a business that I work at each day. Much like the business of new home construction, retail business, membership development, marketing, or ownership, each of our life experiences teach us something worth knowing, and so often something we needed to learn. Many times, our life pursuits teach us what we are here to learn as human beings even when we believe it's simply about a job or a career pursuit.

Your education, and soon your college selection, will have everything to do with learning new things which will expand your horizons and knowledge and awareness of who you are and what it is that you are here on earth for and what you hope to accomplish while you are here. I believe that we choose our destinies as we travel down different pathways of life, either very carefully or recklessly, but as our choice.

When we reach a point where we are uncertain which road to take, it is at that time we must deliberate, pray, and seek higher understanding and assistance to choose a better way for us to continue our journey.

For if we are only granted that knowledge that we have gained up to that crossroads in our life, then we are very limited, as a rule, as to the amount of knowledge that we personally have to make a well-informed and good decision. This is why I believe that we have friends, loved ones, and family to help support us and act as instruments for us to gain added information and perspective to help us make our best decisions all throughout our life wherever we may go.

In a beautiful song that I listened to again today, called, "Have I Told You Lately," by Van Morrison, the words "Ah, the morning sun and all its glory, fills the day with hope and constitute, you fill my life with laughter and you make it better... you ease my troubles, that's what you do," and those words echo my true feelings and sentiments for you and Mother.

I once signed a marriage vow to love your mother always and forever. How little did I know then that I not only would have no problems doing that, but that it would grow better and stronger with each passing hour that we are together. The same is true with you.

"Have I told you lately how much I love you?" is more than a song to me. It's a way of life. I love you, and you have grown to be one of my closest confidants and friends. I knew that you would always be my son, but I had no idea that we could ever be such good friends.

When I do something that you don't care for or appreciate as much, please remember: I'm more than just a father to you. I am someone who holds you in the highest esteem always...and forever.

That's just how it is, son. I hope you always realize your dreams and ambitions and keep up the excellent work and effort. It will all mean something as you go forward each day.

If you're lucky, one day you'll meet someone you'll love every bit as much or more than the love your mother and you and I know together as a family. That's when you'll realize how precious time really is.

Love, Dad

And then there is this letter that will share another perspective on how I felt and what I was feeling, approximately one year prior to his passing:

"Defining our Life"

From the earliest records discovered recording the events of mankind through today, man has always sought to define another man by one or several events of a lifetime. We do this as human beings to simplify our reasoning and our recall processes so that the events which we elect to think about are shorter and easier or summarizing to our life.

But the truth of our lives are not found in just this one or two characterizations about us. The truth of our life is the discovery of each moment of each new day and all that it has to offer to us.

How we choose to remember life is based on how we feel about life at any given moment. When we recall happiness, we see one or multiple events that shaped our momentary thoughts, experiences, feelings, and emotions. But life is far more than this.

Life is a collection of dreams, acts, actions, thoughts, emotions, and spiritual quests. It is a day-to-day, carousel of unfolding drama and events that never really stop even when we pass on from this earth.

Life is too complex in this way for us to fully grasp how it continues and never truly ends. We simplify our memories and reminisce about those things that most often teach us the most about life. For those things remind us of what we needed to know at the time that we experienced these events.

Gary Vaught

When we want to look forward, we single out goals and ambitions and give our life energy to these. When we want to live for the day or the moment, we elect to be with the here-and-now so that we can cherish what it is that we have at this time. When we choose to look back over our lives, we are seeking to remember those events that defined who we are, what we are, and how we have lived our life.

But we must remember that we are and always will be much, much, more than simple defining moments. We are tapestries still as a work in process...sewing the fabric of our spiritual existence with our needs, our wants, and our truths as we know them.

The quilt of life is the blanket that we create to cover our spirit and still expose our barren and precious self, and that which we were, we are, and we will continue to be and become.

Life is never over. It is a transition from what we have known to what we are about to discover. Because we fear uncertainties, it is basic human response that we are without the preparation it seems sometimes to move on when our time has come to move on.

But this is where our defining moments give us strength, courage, hope, and faith that we are indeed prepared (whether we realize it or not).

We never walk alone. We never walk separate paths. We just choose to look inward many times, rather than about us to see what is before us, around us, and behind us. Every one of us will walk into the future together. It is a daily and continuous procession of life. We will not walk alone...we will walk with others knowingly or unknowingly in the celebration of our continued life.

How we choose to remember ourselves is up to us. We are always with our true self and yet, it is understood that we must simplify our recollection and memories for there are so many...to more simply understand our life, and our meaning for our life.

I choose to remember that all of us are here today and somewhere else tomorrow. But we can and will take with us the precious memories as a means of never forgetting the past. But so can we take our future dreams and goals and live these even when we change living spaces. Wherever it is that we want to call home, we will always have the freedom to have the moment, the future, and the past.

But our life is a composition, not a single event. We created our own tapestry to help us remind oneself and others of who we wanted to be at any given moment.

Say goodbye if that is comforting to you. But please remember that this is a parade and it never ends...we just need rest sometimes, to get back up and join in again.

Gary Vaught

In our communications which followed the week after Gabriel's funeral, he literally told me that this particular letter of "Defining Our Life" was a literal communication, as well as a figurative translation of what occurs not only here on earth, but during different segments throughout one's transition to the other side, and then life forever after.

How could I remember this? Why did I choose to write this to him? What was the purpose of the timing for this? Did someone else assist me without my realizing it? If so, why?

One of the most impressionable early thoughts that Gabe communicated to us was that there are parades every day where he currently resides. That it is a continuous procession of life and that those present can see the past, present, and future. Certain spirits do need rest when first transitioning to the other side. But soon, they get back up and join in again when that rest has provided enough energy for them to do so.

He spoke of his personal transition, at the moment of his passing from earth, as one that allowed him and others to pass over together at the same time.

I was amazed at how insightful that letter was in the literal sense. I still cannot fathom how I wrote this or why. Gabe has told me repeatedly though, "not one single encounter or event on earth is an accident. It is all planned and part of each person's destiny, down to the very nanosecond of life on earth."

In looking back over all the letters and seeing how I shared my feelings with my son before he transitioned from the physical to the spiritual afterlife, I realize that my higher consciousness had to have played a part in every one of these moments where I was inspired to write these prophetic letters. My subconscious mind was allowing me to recall so many things that I would need to recall in order to be better prepared for the time when our son would no longer be here physically, and perhaps, remind myself of the fact that life goes on here and hereafter.

If I had not had this time to grieve or had not taken this approach in the years leading up to Gabriel's passing from earth, I am uncertain that either my wife or I would have survived this ordeal, because we would have both been too deeply depressed to have been able to continue on without one of us being able to support the other. In that respect, it has been a true blessing for us.

I now give all thanks to God and Glory be to God for each new day and each opportunity to not only experience the sadness that I still feel, but to work through it throughout different periods of each day, each week.

For the many wonderful people who come to comfort us, be with us, and send their love and support to us, and who have said so many kind words and prayers on our behalf, I am truly grateful! For we feel these so deeply in our souls.

The combination of all of these things that has made it possible for us to get through these painful and difficult days immediately following his passing from the physical plane of existence that he calls "the teaching zone" is what inspires us to look ahead with knowledge that we have grown stronger through these trials.

We've learned so much in such a short time and we continue to learn each day. I am so grateful for all the blessed messages of hope, opportunity, peace, and beauty that come our way even during the midst of what can truly be described as our single greatest family tragedy.

The blessed communications from Gabe now are far greater than anything we could have anticipated upon our arrival at Saint Xavier the night we found his physical body lying dead to the world.

I know that Gabe has a plan, and God has a plan, and although I don't understand any of it in its entirety, I hope to step into the "flow of life" to the largest possible extent each and every day encouraging my spirit to live a better life through the blessed messages that we still receive.

My son once told me while he was in high school that he had very few friends who truly cared about him. Nearly six hundred people showed up to give their support to us in a twenty-four-hour period of time between the Thursday visitation and Friday funeral service. Some may have come to comfort us, but most came to honor him and pay their final respects to him. He was their friend.

Among all of the people who attended the service, there was a chartered busload of students and faculty who drove down from Saint Xavier University, a three-and-a-half-hour drive, (not including the time needed to repair a flat tire), to pay their respects to a young man they'd only known a short time — less than eight months.

Our son grew and was nurtured in such a wonderful God-centered environment at Saint Xavier University in Chicago. The school will forever be in our hearts and we hope to help them in every way that we can so that other parents will learn how balanced and wonderful the university truly is.

The entire University family has been so caring and giving, even two years later. From prayer vigils, to chapel services, to radio tribute shows on WXAV 88.3 FM in Chicago, to the honor of the September 15, 2004, campus-wide memorial service for Gabe. This has been nothing less than remarkable, seeing the outpouring of love and affection for one of their own. SXU is a place anyone can feel great about sending their child on to for advanced education.

My son truly appreciated his final weeks and months at Saint Xavier University and part of our peace with this whole thing is in knowing that of all the places that he could have physically passed away at on earth, that he was in God's hands at this God-centered institution, surrounded by so many caring people who loved him and accepted him for who he was —not who they wanted him to be. All are and will continue to be a part of his extended family of friends here; and hereafter, I am certain!

From the security guards, to the faculty, to the students at his dormitory at Regina Hall, to classmates who didn't even really know him, we received so many loving and kind thoughts and expressions of consideration. I can easily say it was overwhelming at times. Overwhelmingly beautiful…to my wife, to me, and to our son, in spirit, who has confirmed this information to us already. He wanted to let others know of the power of caring for others, even in transition to the other side! Love's expressions are felt throughout the entire universe when they occur. They raise the universal consciousness and brighten the possibilities for a better universe each moment.

In a rare moment of humor one night, when tears were streaming from my wife's eyes and my eyes while conversing with him in the afterlife, he said humorously "…and to think that all I had to do was die to become famous." I thought to myself *"what a price to pay, son, for any small amount of fame that you may have earned."* And, he knew what he was saying was only half-hearted for any recognition brought to him is appreciated, however, totally insignificant now. He has since made that abundantly clear.

He is not in this afterlife to win awards, or influence skeptics, or to perform magic tricks for doubters, but "to enable understanding and inspire hope in those who have so little." He has a much greater job to do — and little interest in wasting time despite the fact that time has no meaning in his "diagram" (dimension of his soul)!

Gabe sharing a special moment displaying his tenderness by feeding the animals at the Pumpkin patch Petting Zoo with his second cousin Alexa

Gabe on a spring vacation in San Diego CA during his senior year

CHAPTER ELEVEN

Receiving the Medical Report from the Medical Examiner in Chicago

On Saturday, June 26, 2004, Dawn and I finally received the much-awaited and anticipated final medical report from the medical examiner's office from Cook County out of Chicago regarding our son's cause of death. By the time we received this report, it had been nine weeks and we had gotten to the point where our communications with Gabe had really convinced us that it was less and less important for us to understand how he passed away and much more important for us to understand the purpose for it. Once any of us pass on, the details of the passing are really a passing matter. The moment is all that we can live in; here, or hereafter.

Still, Dawn and I could not bring final closure to this in any possible way without understanding that which actually took place that led to the death of our son. So, even though Gabriel in his after life communication with us continued to tell us that it was best that we not worry about such things and not concern ourselves with such things, and that we should spend our energy living in the spirit of Christ now, that was hardly our only objective.

He asked us to give more love to one another and to all others who we come into contact with. He said to look for ways to spread kindness, compassion, and good will to the earth, as it was really lacking these essential elements now. Still, we needed this information for our own satisfaction and to provide us with some closure with this.

Neither Dawn nor I are capable of comprehensively translating the medical examiner's report in any great detail. My only experience with this was reading medical reports with my previous occupation as a insurance claims investigator dealing with coroner's reports associated with fatalities resulting from accidents. Medical jargon just isn't a part of my intelligence center.

What did surprise me was that Gabriel was discovered to have arteriosclerosis at such an early age. The medical report diagnosed him as having had as much as fifty-percent closure in one major vessel leading to the heart. Strangely enough, on *CNN News*, I had seen a news banner about three weeks earlier that indicated that any children who had diabetes from an early age should have regular examinations from the age of sixteen on for the potential symptoms of heart disease. This is a very serious matter and one that is becoming a particular concern.

Medical scientists are learning that the rigidity of the vessels leading to and from the heart is a significant concern with diabetics over a prolonged period of time from early youth. This leads to a narrowing of the passages and permits plaque build up, making it far more difficult to treat unless it is diagnosed early on.

Dawn and I asked our family doctor to review the findings, and we telephoned a family friend and former endocrinologist whom Gabe had seen for many years. We were particularly concerned with alternatives as to "the probable cause of death which was determined to be ketoacidosis's meaning, elevated glucose-level-producing ketones that shut the body down.

We both had a hard time understanding how his glucose level so suddenly accelerated when less than twenty-four hours earlier his glucose monitor (tester) indicated that his glucose level was at 282 (high, but not fatal).

No doubt there could be other possibilities because one of his lungs weighed approximately twice what the other one did and there was a significant amount of green bile buildup in his stomach and other areas, reflecting that the likelihood was that he had been sick for a while and probably had very little food consumption. He may or may not have been taking his shots as regularly prescribed as a result of how ill he had become so quickly.

Obviously, he would have tried to adjust his shot frequency as well as the amount of the insulin he was taking to offset the lack of food intake during his illness. That's a very dangerous guessing game at best without a doctor's recommendations. Normally, even doctors and specialists have a very difficult time managing that type of scenario with any real precision.

I still go back to my son's earliest words from the earliest communications that we had after he had died. He stated very factually in an expression that was almost uncharacteristic of him, with a point that he wanted to make with us all the same: *"My number was up, Dad!"*

I believe this means that on April 23, 2004, at the time that he passed on, he could have been anywhere in the world doing anything and it would have been his time to transition to the spirit world.

What was probably the most significant mystery of all (and one that may never be answered in its entirety or accurately, since very few people had contact with Gabriel during the last few hours of his life) was how did Gabe die without our sensing it? Not knowing that he was sick or communicating with him to learn about the illness allowed it to take the course that resulted in his death.

We had never missed these premonitions, messages, or intuitive mental transmissions before. We had sensitized ourselves to him in all ways, especially with the closeness of my intuitive mental powers with Gabe and vice-versa.

I would wake up on a moment's notice at night and know instinctively that something was wrong without Gabe making a sound, from the time he was three years old. And I did hundreds and hundreds of times during his life (at night, primarily).

None of the students who attended Saint Xavier University with Gabe had any real knowledge of the effects of the chronic illness that he had. Type-1 diabetes is something that causes silent suffering from such an extreme illness as a bacterial infection, or what we had thought to be food poisoning from the Wednesday before he passed away the following Friday. From forty-eight hours prior to his death until his passing, no one picked up on any of the clues. No one understood the seriousness of his illness.

This just made the mystery that much greater to me. Most students would not have known what to look for or how to treat diabetes unless they had known someone personally who had experienced it in their lifetime.

Fortunately, since Gabe's death, the university has instituted several chronic illness awareness programs through their school of nursing to help students identify the symptoms and causes of various illnesses. If anyone had truly known about his condition and illness, it seems that someone would have recommended medical treatment or contacted an authority. It was not meant to be. No one could have prevented this ending with all of these circumstances that resulted from the life event..

Gabriel had telephoned some friends and expressed to them that he had felt ill. In one case, he spoke to a friend as he attempted to still attend classes through the day he died. We would later learn from Gabe in one afterlife communication that all the messages were somehow blocked so no one could prevent the finality of his passing at the time he was meant to pass on. This was part of the necessity of the contract.

There is, however, another significant mystery which hangs like a dark cloud over my thoughts and perceptions still, to this day, about his passing. In three different readings (with three different mediums), received information stating that there was no indication of any foul play whatsoever. But because Gabriel's passing was unattended, and so mysterious, I could not help but think about the possibility of that as a potential concern to me. I would have given that little or no credence to that hypothesis at all, but early on after Gabriel's passing (the Saturday following his service), I was coming back from an errand in my car near my home when I was contacted by Gabriel. While driving my automobile, I received very clear communications and I recall hearing very well the message that I would be very proud of him when I learned of something that he was involved with that no one to speak of had any knowledge of and that would come to light by the end of 2004. Although I shared this unusual thought process with my wife later in the day, I hardly think she was in any frame of mind to give my thoughts any real attention at that time.

In questioning him further about this as I drove up the hill leading to our home (not certain if I was talking with myself or going crazy somehow), the only information I received was that he was working on behalf of our government, assisting them in an investigation of some type and that he could not give us any further details at this time, but was hoping that in the future, as time progressed, others would step forward to talk to us about this or that he would be able to reveal those details as appropriate.

I might have thought this to be a figment of my imagination and dismissed this over a short period of time had I not come home that evening after telling my wife of this amazing communications and discovered that, as she was cleaning out many of his albums and CDs from a container that he kept them in, she ran across three large folders, the first of which was labeled "Exceptional Careers US Customs Service." I opened it up and it talked about everything from criminal investigators and special agents, to chemists, to import specialists of customs inspectors, and it talked about all the educational possibilities and superior academic achievements required to join this level of service to our government.

Then I noticed a second folder that was marked "Department of the Treasury - Bureau of Alcohol, Tobacco, and Firearms, Career Opportunities," and on the front it said "Working for a Sound and Safer America Through Innovation of Partnerships." As I opened this up, I saw that it not only gave the history of the ATF, but it talked about how they recruit people and what type of scholars are required to become part of the US Department of Treasury.

To my amazement, there was a third folder from Moraine Valley Community College (in nearby Alsip, Illinois, not far from where Gabe attended Saint Xavier University). Inside this folder, we found information that was quite personal including the social security number and identity of another individual dating back to several years previously.

Complete with that information was a number of academic success checklists and orientation quiz questions and program study requirements, including trial class schedules for what appeared to be criminal justice programming through that school. None of this made any sense to me and it wouldn't for many months.

When I asked Gabe for more information, he refused to go into any great detail — or to deny any of the facts. He only stated that when it's possible, he will relate additional details but that the investigation is still underway and he is not at liberty to give us any further information. When I tried using my investigation background from my insurance claims investigation days, I was able to pick up a few small clues that led me to suspicious questions about phone activity and contact activity that he may have had in the (forty-eight hours) days leading up to his death. I thought it necessary to discuss this with him. It was my business as his father to see where this was taking us.

His comments were, "Stay out of this, Dad; it doesn't concern you. Leave this to people who know what they are doing. Dad, you are better off affecting the world in a positive way than trying to pick up on an investigation that you know nothing about and have no business being involved with."

I went to a medium at Camp Chesterfield (near Muncie, Indiana) to see if I could get confirmation of whether this information was accurate or if we were still imagining this and an eighty-year-old clairvoyant and medium whom I had come to trust and had used many times over the past fifteen years summoned enough energy to refer me to her next door neighbor who I had seen over that same period of time and was willing to discuss the matter in greater detail with us.

She indicated that Gabriel had been reporting to three men (whose names I will not disclose because I first of all, I did not get their accurate names, and secondly, I only received information on what either their code names were or what their duties and responsibilities appeared to be, and I do not wish to reveal this information at this time until I am certain that it is of no consequence one way or the other to any investigation that may be underway at this time). However, one of the men was a very high-ranking official in Washington, D.C., another handled money and was out of Chicago, and the third individual was out of the Cleveland area.

It was hard for me to give up this investigation because I naturally wanted to know all that I could about my son's life and especially that which I had no knowledge of that may have at some point in time influenced his life (or death, possibly). Still, everyone assured me there was no foul play in his death (including Gabe on three occasions).

So, in my follow-up conversations with Gabe, I continued to probe, even though I could tell it was irritating to him to a small degree that I continued to bring this up. Yet, I had to think that he brought this to my attention for a certain reason. Approximately nine months later, Gabe told me one evening that he had been working on an undercover assignment to aid authorities in catching a drug dealer who had sold bad substances that had taken the life of two kids he had met through his music appreciation in Chicago.

This knowledge I could be very proud of. The fact that he cared enough to risk his life to capture someone taking others' lives was heartwarming, after the fact. Maybe it was his way of showing us that he had achieved true independence with his life before he passed away; I really don't know. He may have just wanted us to know that he did other things with his energies and concerns for others.

There was some reason that he felt it was not in our best interest to know any more of the details. Perhaps he feared that I would become involved and not fulfill my true destiny by trying to become involved in affairs that did not require my involvement..

The entire matter is one that still leaves me uncomfortable and wanting for more details. But I will likely never know any more than what he has chosen to tell us. The past now belongs to the past.

The Cook County medical examiner's report indicated that Gabriel died from natural causes due to ketoacidosis, and we will have no choice but to accept this now unless we care to have Gabe's body exhumed and another autopsy performed. At this point, I'm not sure what that would accomplish and our son is telling us to move on and not spend any more energy or our valuable time or money on doing this.

I still wonder to this day how he could have possibly have led a life that would have allowed one free moment from his studies, his radio involvement, or his investment of his time to the community with any special project volunteer work.

He had several personal relationships and along with his dorm friendship time, and travels to and from our home, he seemed to always be busy. He performed music production work and worked as a DJ at private parties. He used his time efficiently, I'd say. He made the most of the time that he had given to him.

The greatest mystery to me is that Gabriel went through a significant amount of money that he had earned from working for more than two years prior to college (at a restaurant called The Garrison, in Lawrence, Indiana).

Gabe was the most conservative-minded youngster on the earth at times and actually saved ten thousand dollars during the last two years of high school, for his first semester of his freshman year at Xavier.

Still, he was completely broke after Christmas of his freshman year and the beginning of his second semester of his freshman year. We only gave him four hundred dollars total cash between January 1, 2004 and April 23, 2004, and somehow he managed to come home several times in between that period of time and never required anything else of us whatsoever, despite our offers to give him money. He had no income, to our knowledge, because he wasn't working consistently as a DJ.

It is difficult for me to understand how he could have lived on this amount of income for that period of time when the first semester of his freshman year he needed more than twenty-five times that amount for him to get by. But when I would ask him if he needed money, he would say "No, I'm fine, I have twenty, thirty, or forty dollars," and I would always think to myself that he had enough to get by for now and I assumed that when money grew short, I'd hear from him again. It did not happen.

Upon his passing, I checked his bank account and closed that account and discovered that he had only five dollars to his name. In his room, immediately following his passing, he had only five dollars to his name in cash.

There was no other money discovered or located anywhere else in his possession. I was deeply concerned and distressed upon learning that he only had ten dollars to his name when he passed away and felt very guilty initially about this.

Why didn't I know that he was running so low and why wouldn't he have told us as usual when he needed money for something? The whole thing seemed wildly unbelievable, and Gabe had never had a problem asking us for a loan or simply a grant if he needed money for something that he truly wanted or had to have for school.

As this mystery continued to unfold, and I thought about the fact that he indicated he was being paid for the work that he was doing for our country, I had to wonder if he had spent that money or it was invested in a separate account that we'll never know anything about, somewhere else in the world. Who knows?

While visiting this very enlightened and gifted medium at Camp Chesterfield, IN, we had many questions about our son's life, but the one that stood out in my mind the most was when I asked her, "Was there anything that our son was doing that we didn't have knowledge of?"

She smiled and said, "Your son had many sets of friends and people that he associated with that you had no knowledge of whatsoever. He had so many interests and pursued so many things in his life that you could not possibly have stayed up with all of the people that he knew, met, or associated with, because he was always involving himself with new and different people. They came from all walks of life and some were not so desirable from your life expectations of his friends. Others were simply outstanding people just like your son. He liked diversity. He enjoyed the many different types of people and the many different levels of people that he associated with periodically. He found great learning experiences through all of these associations, apparently. They helped him in learning his lessons here on earth".

It is a wonder that someone so young — eighteen — could have lived such a full life and a life that had so many different aspects to it. As his parents who loved him so deeply and thought we knew him so completely, we wonder how we could have so little idea of how significantly his actions were impacting the world around him. From his efforts with his peer group at Lawrence North High School (even after he left there to attend Saint Xavier University) to his efforts at Saint Xavier University to complete an extraordinary freshman year, complete with a 4.0 grade point average and honors of all types, to building new relationships in Chicago.And, he had traveled to so many other places throughout the school year, to visit friends and meet new people. Then the matter of doing work on behalf of our government in assisting them, with all of this it just seemed so difficult to grasp.

Gabe's High School Graduation Cake in 2003 (graduated from Lawrence North High School in Indianapolis, IN, receiving an academic scholarship to attend Saint Xavier University in Chicago, IL)

Gabe's last summer celebration with his family at the 500 Mile Race Memorial Day celebration held at cousin Kim's farm near Cicero, IN

Chapter Twelve

·Glory Be to God

.I will always aspire to continue to learn and to gather truth and have learned to start listening to all children more carefully.: "For out of the mouths of babes," my son included. their examples are there waiting to teach us quite often what we may have not learned yet. Or, perhaps, learned and simply forgotten in time.

They have a closer link to God as they typically remember their Higher Purpose for their lifetime and His part in it to a larger degree subconsciously!

I thank God for all the lessons and learning experiences that lie ahead of both my wife and I.. The unknown is so inspiring and beautiful for what it brings to us as it passes over to become our own personal life experiences..

In our deepest and darkest moments of sorrow, following the passing of our son, we continue to learn from our many experiences each day.

Gabe is always there to help us better understand our "life missions." He watches our lives now as we would a videotape, only he sees it all in "real time," he tells us. When he so chooses to be a part of something that we do as a family, he joins in and we never fail to experience his spirited energy with us. It's natural to us now and we know when he is with us or elsewhere in the space-time continuum for all of life.

I learned from Gabe shortly after our afterlife conversations began that I had started to prepare myself through my higher awareness (consciousness) for his impending death. It is so hard to comprehend. I have read previously, and heard through Gabe — that each of us retain an awareness of our life-and-death contracts at the highest level of awareness in our existence.

That being said, we don't typically have the ability to tap into our higher self when we are on earth due to earthly limitations that keep us in the "here and now." Still, some people are capable of sensing certain characteristics about their eternal life experiences, including those that have yet to occur physically (i.e., *deja vu* experiences that we have all felt and experienced at some point in our life).

After looking back at many letters that I had written to Gabe more than two years earlier,(prior to his death), it becomes remarkably prophetic to see how I was preparing myself and Gabe for the future transition we both were to experience.

Again, I give all Glory to God for all of these lessons and those that remain ahead of us. And, I give so much credit to my son for the eighteen precious years we had to share together here and to learn so much from him both here and from the hereafter!

The fact that he has never quit caring for human kind, despite the fact that he left it in our care to manage, nearly two years ago, is a testament in my opinion as to how the spirit of God plays out in the work that is done in the afterlife.

His continuous love and support still help us to continue healing today. We still both see the world with different perspectives at times. However, I have every reason to believe that he sees it more clearly for what it truly is now, while many times, I simply muddle through with my limited knowledge and enlightenment!

These past two years have been the most rewarding years of my life. Since his transition, nothing I have ever learned independently has even remotely taught me so much about my actions and my responsibilities in life as his communications and his continued concern for me.

The afterlife is so blessed with Light and Light decision-making. Our world is so full of illusion.

As we continue with our healing, this book and the truth as it is known to us keep me optimistic about the future of our world. One of Gabe's afterlife missions was to instill hope in us, when we had so little left, he stated.

From my standpoint, he more than succeeded. He has brought new awareness to me and to anyone else who can stand before God and profess their faith in the afterlife. For there the truth is, through our highest calling, and not our ego-based ambitions.

I simply believed and was granted the immense blessing of his communications with us. Through divine guidance and promise, and our faith in our ability to achieve these communications with our deceased loved ones, we can all learn from afterlife spirits while we are still living here in the "teaching zone" to some degree.

They want to let us know how well they live, too, and that they are still apart of us and vice-versa! Why would we want to shut them out?

Perhaps one day, my prayers will allow me to transition to their side with the knowledge that I cared and I believed, while so few on earth would even desire to do so.

My hope is that somehow, perhaps, some of you will change your mindsets after reading my story. I hope that you will allow yourselves the opportunity to learn what I have learned so far. There aren't classes typically provided on teaching *good common sense*... But, if there were, an absolute prerequisite would be to consult with higher forms of life.

I have been asked, "How many people are blessed with this opportunity to listen, to share in this type of understanding, and to realize that their deceased loved ones are really nearby whenever we simply think of them, or they somehow cross our mind?"

The answer is the same: "Every human being who learns to trust their inner voice, believe in a self-dictated reality, and listen for the music of soulful (spirit) transmissions and feelings of love, can and will experience what I am experiencing, to a certain degree. The question will remain, can you believe in this? It will be up to each of you to answer that question for yourselves.

It may take thousands of years before man can fully comprehend this divine gateway that exists and has for longer than anyone can know.

Yet, until man actually believes in his or her untapped capabilities with all of his or her heart and soul, we will remain less enlightened and less at peace with our soul, making life so much less than what it can be for us, individually and collectively.

We cannot discount knowledge, once we receive it, without great consequences and disadvantages to our opportunities for self peace.

In John Lennon's legendary song, "Imagine," we find some real truths. For those that want to believe, this is a beautiful place to begin to listen to the music!

"Imagine your loved ones are still here with you!"

For when you do that, you acknowledge their existence and permit their involvement on a conscious level into your life here.. Always consider that, in the absence of true knowledge, faith is all that there is for any of us to grow by.

On a note of inspiration, and to bring to a conclusion the thoughts I have expressed here in this book of universal altruisms, I thank my son for his continued support and love that he still sends to us; though, thank you is hardly enough!

I send my fullest, heartfelt love back to you and remind you of how much God has blessed you and me as we continue our individual journey's through our own realities.

As Einstein has said, *"The intellect has little to do on the road to discovery. There comes a leap in consciousness, call it intuition or what you will, the solution comes to you and you don't know how or why."*

That is enough…for now!

With all my love for you, I remain your…

Dad

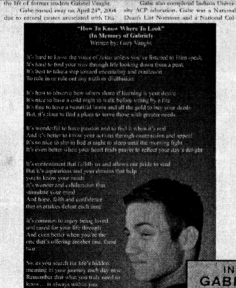

Gabe's University Newspaper "The Xavierette", remembering his memory at the special campus memorial in September of 04', placed at Saint Xavier University in front of Regina hall, forever honoring his accomplishments as a student, a friend, and a WXAV radio broadcaster. The poem was written and read by Gary, as a final rites eulogy, honoring everyone at the University and Gabe's time and efforts there.

Gabe's monument placed upon his grave at Hamilton Memorial Cemetery near Noblesville, IN.

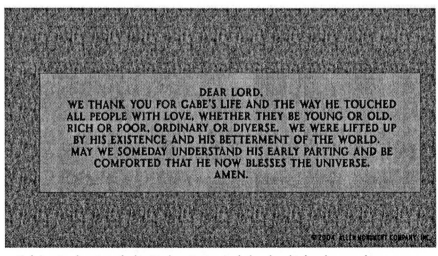

Gabe's epitaph written by his Mother, Dawn, and placed on his bench seat at his monument

The very first Saint Xavier, "Gabriel Vaught Memorial Scholarship" award winner, honored in 2005, (Mr. Peter Kreten), along with Dawn and Gary Vaught, at the awards celebration in Chicago.

Gary Vaught is a self-employed businessman that has worked throughout his life in marketing and sales, predominantly. He has accomplished many goals in his life, yet, felt the overwhelming need to publicly share the intimate details of his eighteen year old son, Gabriel's, premature death.

Gabriel's inspirational contact with his family through Dawn (his mother and channel medium), and Gary, his father, only two days following his transition to the other side of life, is incredible and miraculous.

Gabriel's messages contain Divine information that is being brought to the earth for the first time, in some cases. Other messages contain quality of life principles found on earth and in the hereafter. Because of the extraordinary nature of so many of these messages, Gary was directed to publish this book, "My Number Was Up, Dad", despite much resistance from those that could not comprehend or accept his extraordinary change of life for him.

Gary learned through Divine guidance and communications that he had many seeds to plant and to cultivate as his life mission following the numerous conversations that he had with his son, and Jesus Christ.

Gary has never been a deeply religious person and does not belong to any denomination of religious order or faith. He does hold a combination of Christian and Judaic and Buddhist principles as his guiding lights for living on earth. Not until the tragic death of his son on April 23, 2004, did he contemplate his higher purpose and reason for continuing to live.

In a period of deep sadness and grief, he knelt to pray to God for understanding and enlightenment on why his son had to be taken at such an early age. God answered through Jesus Christ and a series of revelations regarding the synchronicity of Gabriel and Gary's life's that are still unfolding beyond anyone's imaginations.

Gary opened his heart and his mind and listened to the words of each and every Divine Spirit that talked with him in the weeks and months and year to come, through Gabriel. Through these magnificent prophecies, revelations, quests, and objectives, he found a new purpose that had long awaited his arrival, though through the most suddenly tragic and difficult period of his life.

His love for his son and his Maker provided a continuous unfolding of "need to know information"

that is meant for delivering to the world that will listen. As a "messenger of faith", an earth given identity described by Jesus in a one hour detailed conversation early on, Gary learned that he had a long road ahead full of challenges, sacrifices, and, yet much joy and love.

He accepted the work that he was blessed to do and now shares his inspiration for these personal messages and direct messages delivered to him by Christ. Never really knowing what will come next in his life, he awakens each day to listen to the call from his Providers. Gary acts on the calls and carries out the work that he feels so honored to share.

In this book, he provides messages of hope, faith, love, creation, Godliness, and facts about life here on earth and hereafter. He never questions the messages, although on numerous occasions he questions himself. Why is he so blessed to have the opportunity to spread hope and goodwill, wherever he is called to be?

The answers, that will be answered at this time, lie in the book and in the hands of God who only really knows the Divine picture for all of this. Gary's life will never be the same. The messages enlighten all who choose to listen. Life alternatives then become a possibility for change as inevitably the world receives these messages and spiritual guidance on a level that is easily understood.

Printed in the United States
58853LVS00008B/142-195

9 781425 937867